4 X 1|11 √2/12

D0933996

WITHDRAWN

THE STICKING POINT
SOLUTION

THE STICKING POINT
SOLUTION

**9 Ways to Move Your Business
from Stagnation to Stunning Growth
in Tough Economic Times**

JAY ABRAHAM

Vanguard Press
A Member of the Perseus Books Group

Designed by Pauline Brown
Set in 11 point Sabon

Cataloging-in-Publication data for this book are available from the Library of Congress.
ISBN-13: 978-1-59315-510-0

Vanguard Press books are available at special discounts for bulk purchases in the U.S. by corporations, institutions, and other organizations. For more information, please contact the Special Markets Department at the Perseus Books Group, 2300 Chestnut Street, Suite 200, Philadelphia, PA 19103, or call (800) 810-4145, ext. 5000, or e-mail special.markets@perseusbooks.com.

10 9 8 7 6 5 4 3 2 1

CONTENTS

ACKNOWLEDGMENTS

I'm just egotistical enough to tell you that this is the book that will make the difference for you between failure and success in this post-2008 crisis economy—and beyond.

On the other hand, I'm not so egotistical as to suggest that every one of the hundreds of approaches, strategies, and tactics described herein were invented by the author. Instead, you'll find in these pages the ideas (duly acknowledged, of course!) of some of the most brilliant business minds in the world today—men and women who are not just legendary figures in the worlds of marketing and sales but also my friends, colleagues, co-authors, and co-presenters, and current and past business strategic partners. First among equals is Rich Schefren, whose brilliance enlivens many of the chapters of this book, and without whom the book (and many successful online marketers) would be immeasurably poorer.

You'll also discover the ideas of Chet Holmes, with whom I have repeatedly shared the speaker's platform and whose book, *The Ultimate Sales Machine*, I endorse heartily.

And the ideas of Andy Miller, a genius when it comes to consultative selling.

Thank you, Barbara Lowenstein, for agenting the deal and selling the book in so many foreign markets.

A special thank you also goes to Roger Cooper, the publisher, for his faith in this book and his willingness to roll up his sleeves and make it a success.

To Ruth Mills, who ably copyedited the book, helping me to sound more organized and concise than is often the case in real life. To Michael Levin, who—though he takes life, and me, too seriously—gave my ideas a stronger, clearer voice.

To Christy, who has been after me for years to write another book.

And to all the wonderful people who have taken me under their wing over the last thirty years to counsel, mentor, teach, and train me in all their wisdom and knowledge.

If I have failed to acknowledge anyone else in this book for their ideas and influence, it's merely an unintentional oversight and for that, I duly apologize.

This book is offered to business owners, entrepreneurs, professionals, start-ups, and managers alike, with the hope that it will help your respective enterprises keep going, growing, and thriving in this bad economy and beyond.

BAD ECONOMY? GOOD NEWS!

I love a bad economy.

So do my clients.

And after you read this book, so will you.

For all the pain they cause, economic downturns—like the one we're in today—allow us to discover that areas of growth are actually more plentiful in hard times than in boom times. And that's why I appreciate such downturns.

In a bad economy, you can walk all over your competition, lap the field, run circles—you pick the metaphor. The main thing is that you can win easily—if you know how to benefit from bad times. Everyone else is dropping out of the race, and you're seeing the checkered flag. Everyone else is looking backward, and you're looking forward. They're terrified, and you're making a fortune. Indeed, you're seeing opportunities and overlooked markets, transactions, and areas of thinking that no one else saw in good times, so they certainly won't see them in times of financial struggle.

The Sticking Point Solution makes a unique promise. Anyone can show you how to succeed when all the indicators are up. But I'm going to show you how to succeed as never before—when the national and global financial picture looks bleak.

As I was completing this book, the stock market's gyrations reached an unprecedented level. On one day in particular, the market dropped more than 700 points. But during the same day, *100 stocks went up*. Why is it that even when the news is at its worst, some companies are having their best year ever?

And why can't you?

You can, and in this book I will show you precisely how.

My starting point is to ask, with all due respect, whether your business or enterprise might be stuck.

A "stuck" business, whether it's entrepreneurial in nature or a Fortune 500 company, is one that fails to grow predictably every year, every quarter, every day. If you're being carried along by the marketplace, then the moment the marketplace dries up, your business is going to dry up, too, because you're not in control of your destiny. In good times, stuck businesses don't even realize they're stuck!

Imagine a business that made $100,000 last year and $110,000 this year. The CEO could argue that the business is growing, but in actuality it may have been the market that has grown—and without any proactive or strategic action on the CEO's part. In such cases, when the market dries up, it takes stuck companies down with it. And the company that once made $110,000 now makes only $70,000. Or less. In the meantime, its competitor (applying the ideas you'll find in this book) is doing $250,000 worth of business.

Why do so many businesses get stuck and stay stuck? The top four reasons for stagnation, in my experience, are the following:

1. not incorporating growth thinking into every aspect of the business;

2. not measuring, monitoring, comparing, or quantifying results;

3. not having a detailed, strategic marketing plan with specific performance growth expectations; and

4. not knowing how to set appropriate, specific goals.

These problems are magnified in tough economic times. First, there's the problem of lower revenue because the business climate is poor. And, second, the very concept of recession or hard times "freezes" people. They get scared. They don't know what to do, so they tend to do nothing, or to do more of the things that weren't working in the first place.

The good news for you is that your competition probably isn't reading *The Sticking Point Solution*. In fact, in difficult economic times like these, it's very likely that your competitor is scurrying to stay afloat or is already out of business, leaving more of the market to you.

The purpose of this book is to show you how to make sure the same thing doesn't happen to you. In fact, I'll go one step further and say that I want to teach you to embrace recessions and economic downturns, and to learn how to profit handsomely from your business challenges and adversities, and even from your competition's missteps. One such misstep is to pack up and leave when the going gets tough. But if you know how to be strategic, how to direct your business or your department intelligently, how to grow and sustain high-profit clients, and how to capitalize on the shortcomings of your competitors, you'll quickly find that you can enjoy even more success and make even more money than you would during so-called boom times.

If your business is stuck, I'll get you unstuck. And by the time you finish *The Sticking Point Solution*, you'll approach tough economic times the same way that many prosperous businesspeople do—by saying, Bring 'em on! You may not love the bad times more than the good ones, but you'll have the confidence that comes with being able to profit, no matter what the economy—or your competition—is doing. You'll see options and opportunities that weren't evident in the past. And you'll have a highly specific action plan to reach stratospheric levels of growth. All of this while the commentators on the financial news networks are wringing their hands daily.

As a business owner or professional, you should be anything but fearful in a bad economy or recessionary period. In a good market, almost all anybody has to do is suit up and wait for business to arrive at the doorstep. The "jet stream" of prosperity carries all businesspeople forward. They don't have to be good at doing business. They don't have to be strategic. They don't have to offer their clients unique advantages. They don't even have to be growth-minded. They just get carried along, willy-nilly. Even those who are inept can grow along with the climbing economic trend.

But in a bad economy, such people become paralyzed. The music stops, and they don't know what to do. They retreat. They stagnate. They spend more time doing more of the same ineffectual things they were doing before, but their ineptitude is no longer disguised by the enormous force of the upward momentum of a positive economy. Such businesses are like hang gliders: Once they get moving, they can go for hours. But when they find themselves buffeted by changes in air pressure beyond their control, their crash landings are scary to watch.

A handful of businesses actually become strategic during hard times. By taking on a growth-minded strategy, these businesses capture the vast majority of new clients in the market—people who weren't already buyers or who weren't ready to move forward, or perhaps didn't previously have the need for a given product or service. But even more important, strategically minded companies capture—or "steal" in an ethical manner, if you will—15 to 20 percent of the best buyers from all of their competitors.

So, if you're attracting all the new buyers in your market *and* you're appropriating, say, 15–20 percent of the best, most profitable, and most repetitive buyers from a half-dozen of your competitors, you're doubling—believe it or not, *doubling*—what you might have accomplished even in an upmarket. For that matter, even if the bottom has fallen out of the economy, or your industry in particular, you can still grow 60, 80, or 100 percent or more while everyone around you is stalling or even failing and collapsing. If you're ready to get serious about understanding value propositions, irresistible offers, and the concept of preemptiveness, along with the other potent concepts I'll share with you in this book, success can be yours in a most tangible, thrilling way.

In this connection, bear in mind that every business has at its disposal twenty to fifty or more highly "upside-leverageable" impact points—or (eX) factors. These (eX) factors can create exponential income if you recognize them and harness them. They increase the likelihood that people will call you or go to your website. They make it easier for you to close sales and deals. They turn one-time buyers into clients who buy every quarter, and they turn nonbuyers into people who buy *something*. These factors are the surprisingly, perhaps even embarrassingly, simple things you can do to bring in more prospects, more sales, more profit, more conversions, more markets, and more ways to start and sustain relationships. If your business has fifty (eX) factors going for it and you increase your effectiveness in, say, just ten of those leverage areas, you will be poised not just to survive in challenging economic times but to thrive as never before. W. Edwards Deming recognized these factors in the manufacturing world and used this knowledge to help develop corporate titans. I've taken the same approach and applied it to something far more important: the revenue-generating process for *your* business.

Again, despite the pain caused by recessions, highly successful, strategic, and totally proactive businesspeople embrace them because hard economic times cleanse the marketplace of marginal competitors who are just reaping the benefits of good times as opposed to being really good businesspeople. That's why I feel comfortable saying that I'm going to teach you to love recessions. You *can* have your best years while those around you are facing disaster. You'll come out of a downturn stronger, more prosperous, and poised to grow faster than you ever hoped, or even imagined.

Business success really is as simple as finding what I call an "under-recognized" or changing need and filling it in with wisdom, empathy, and understanding that no one else can demonstrate or display. In short, you will be solving problems that other people may not even be able to articulate. There are three categories of problems: your own problems, your competitor's problems, and your market's problems. Since time immemorial, the people most skilled at solving the biggest, most important problems have been the best rewarded. That has always been so, and will continue to be.

Chances are that in hard times, both you and your competitors don't even recognize the problems you are struggling with. You might not be able to put these problems into words, let alone find solutions. But if you can get clarity about what problems you're confronting and trying to solve, you can become a master at solving those problems for yourself and for your marketplace. And if you do, rich rewards await you.

Every once in a while, an entrepreneur or company comes along that totally "gets it." Take, for example, JetBlue, the airline that recognized that businesspeople traveling by jet are bored out of their minds. So it installed TVs for every seat on the plane. A simple idea, but a powerful one. Or consider financial adviser and author Howard Ruff, self-styled "champion" of middle-class investors. Having recognized that such investors were being ignored by high-class wealth publications, he made a fortune providing advice to people who weren't rich—yet. American Express also "gets it." It studies peoples' purchasing habits and tailors direct-mail offerings to their likeliest purchases.

One of the prevailing problems I've identified in the marketplace is what I call "ambivalent uncertainty," whereby your client is not just undecided about whether to buy from *you* but unsure whether he should buy *at all*. He's like the person who stands in front of a multiplex, looking at the names of all the movies, unmoved by any of them, unsure whether he really wants to see a movie in the first place. How do you get him to commit to buy a ticket to *your* movie—which then opens up the likelihood that he'll buy popcorn and soda once he gets into the theater, and will buy your movie on DVD a few months later?

Ambivalent uncertainty occurs when your prospects aren't entirely sure that they need your product or service, or aren't completely convinced that you are the right entity to solve their problems. If you can make the most of just these two (eX) factors in your business—by removing your prospects' ambivalence and uncertainty about whether they need what you offer and whether they should choose you over all the rest—enormous success will be yours for the taking.

I'll show you how.

■ ■ ■

So, if being "stuck" is the problem, what needs to happen to get your business unstuck?

You break down your numbers, not just month to month, year to date, and year to year, but also into categories like how many leads and how many new sales by product, average sale, and average product-source. Then, you analyze all of the correlations, implications, and anomalies that these data tell you about.

You have a systematic, strategic process in place that is designed in a predictable, sustainable, and continuous manner to bring in prospects and first-time buyers. You keep advancing and enhancing them forward to recurring purchases in a predictable enough manner that you can look at your numbers today and accurately predict what your business will be like in 90 days, 100 days, or some other time frame. You're able to engineer specific, predictable growth, year after year, because you're zigging while your competitors zag. They're still using direct mail, while you are conducting Webinars and using social media, Internet 2.0, and LinkedIn—things that weren't even on the radar a few years ago. They're running ads that don't pull, while you're tying in with affinity groups who endorse and promote you to their members. And so on.

You are producing not just incremental gains but exponential gains year after year. You achieve this by harnessing the little-understood power of business generating to drive multiplied sales and profits. For example, Costco studied its numbers and realized it made more money by selling memberships than by selling goods in its stores! It now tailors its advertising and marketing to bring people back into the stores to buy things on a regular basis—so they will continue to keep their memberships in good standing. And *The Biggest Loser* TV series promotes The Biggest Loser Club, an online club to which dieters pay a yearly membership fee. More than a million people choose to do so each quarter. Now that's real leverage!

You have clarity about all of the challenges that affect your business, and you realize none of them are insurmountable. In fact, the vast majority can be improved upon. You now see the potential income in any business situation and how to make it work for you in a most enriching manner. For example, you find that you have one category of buyers who are ten times more likely than others to purchase your goods, and if you approach them the right way, they are likely to buy seventeen times more goods than your average client. Or when ads no longer work, you know how to get free media. Or when consumers aren't spending as much money as before, you know how to find alternative propositions to which they can't say no. Or if marketing at corporate events or trade shows stops working for you, you develop a distribution channel none of your competitors know about. You've become Wayne Gretzky, skating to where you know the puck is going to be.

You understand your competitors' appeal, advantage, and differentiation in the market—and you know how to preempt these variables, or to successfully position yourself against them. You learn why certain consumers buy from your competitors and not from you, and you know how to change that.

You know about the alternative products and services that your prospects can buy in lieu of your products and services, including taking no action at all (like our moviegoing friend mentioned earlier). And you can prove to them that choosing *you* represents the most astute decision any buyer could make. You know how to motivate and persuade them to take action and make buying decisions. You enjoy not just what I call a "static awareness," or a theoretical knowledge of your marketplace, but the ability to turn a cool profit through your prospects and clients.

You're incorporating growth thinking into everything you do, every action you take, every investment you make, every contact you forge with your buyer or marketplace. Let's take Kevin Trudeau as an example. Trudeau is famous for his books on memory and health cures. He is also a master of the infomercial. You want to know the secret to his success? Trudeau succeeds because he runs ads *before* he sets prices! He first determines how many inquiry calls per thousand viewers an infomercial has generated—and then sets his pricing accordingly to maximize his profits. That's a brilliant approach. Most people just assume they know how much the market will pay for a product or service, but Trudeau takes the unusual—and highly compelling—step of listening to the market and seeing what it has to say.

These are just a few of the steps you can take to dislodge your business from an awful rut; many more are enumerated on the following pages. Once you know how to tap into the secret wealth of a bad economy, you'll be back on track to superior success. And in this book, I'll show you how.

■ ■ ■

There's one last question you may be asking yourself. Why should you listen to me?

The answer might sound brash—but facts are facts. As Gil Grissom says on *CSI*, "The evidence tells the story." I have more than $7 billion of wealth creation documented for my business clients. I have 12,500 success stories on record. I have something like 3,000 prominent authors and experts who quote me in their published work. My approach is not that of a "nouveau start-up" or "self-proclaimed guru" with an ideological theory that is unproven. On the contrary, I have engineered more successes for more businesses in more industries and in more countries, entrepreneurial or Fortune 500, than just about anyone else on the planet—even in bad times. I have done this for countless people who went from despair to soaring possibilities, and I want to do it for you.

I'm not asking you to pay me $25,000 for a seminar. I'm not asking you to retain me for a six-figure fee and a share of the upside. I'm trying to help you get your business, yourself, your finances, and your life to a better place.

It's the journey of a lifetime. So let's begin.

1

IS YOUR BUSINESS STUCK?

I'm going to share an extraordinary statistic with you: According to my research, 95 percent of all small- and medium-sized businesses and start-ups do not reach their goals. A whopping 95 percent!

That's an awful lot of failure stories. Why? Because most businesses do not have a plan firmly based on four essential factors: product, market, migration, and marketing.

Most businesses lack a concrete, clear picture of where the business is supposed to go. Most business owners simply fail to examine their current projections. They don't ask the "What if?" kinds of questions that lead to staggering success.

They also don't have a copy of *The Sticking Point Solution*. Here's the good news: You do.

My approach will help you avoid this rut. When your company incorporates my strategy, you'll sit down annually to create an integrated, detailed growth plan for the year. Your plan will be broken down backward by product, by market, by marketing, by source, by type of buyer, by month, and sometimes even by week. You'll create strategies that are ready to be invoked right away. You'll monitor and measure the performance of each new strategy every two weeks, if not more often, and when you see deviation down or up, you'll respond pro-actively and immediately, instead of waiting for things to get out of hand.

You'll learn where to get the biggest impact. You'll know what to do, and how to execute on your strategies and tactics. You'll maximize the profitability of your business by replacing unrewarding activities with new concepts you can test right away.

If the deviation is up, you'll be ready to do more in that area. If it's down, you'll adjust by replacing activities, fine-tuning your approach, or adding new lines of attack. This book will give you the guidance you need to make this approach to planning a reality for your business.

What does it feel like to be stuck? It means you're stressed. You're uncertain. You're frustrated. Days go by, and not much happens. You spend an enormous amount of time grappling with unpleasant issues like cash flow or meeting the payroll. It feels like you're hanging from a cliff by your fingernails. You'd like to spend time working on "upside-leverageable" activities, but you aren't sure what the most intelligent steps to take might be. Or if you have some ideas, you aren't sure where to begin or how to execute those ideas. And even if you do know, there are so many daily crises demanding your attention that it's almost impossible to divert energy to strategic projects that could take you to the next level, extricating you from the mental miasma you're trapped in. Profits dry up. Ads don't sell. Prospects don't convert. Margins start dropping. The picture is bleak.

The adage "Grow or die" applies to everything—including the life force of businesses. A business *must* constantly grow. You can't merely be content to survive; you must commit to thriving. In the following pages, I'll show you what to do first, what to do second, and what to do after that—the how to, where to, and why to, so you don't feel as though you've been left stranded with "big-picture" ideas that don't result in a specific plan of action.

You often hear people say that a house is the ultimate investment that most individuals ever make. In reality, however, it is your business where you invest, commit, and spend as much as 80 percent of your waking hours. It is also where your emotions should be invested. It is where your passion should be channeled. It is where your wealth and asset value should be created and meaningfully multiplied. And yet, most entrepreneurs really don't see it that way.

When you invest energy, time, and money in your business, you are creating not just income but real wealth. Why? Because you can sell your business for anywhere from five to fifteen times earnings, depending on your field. Nothing else can possibly touch that level of return. And by relieving yourself of all the stress you feel, you'll be loved even more by your family, too!

In my opinion, you not only deserve the maximum current and future payout from your business; you should *expect* it, in both tangible and intangible forms. You deserve more success, a constantly expanding income, total certainty, a high net worth, and all the perks of success. Yes, I'm referring to financial wealth here, but that brings with it satisfaction, gratification, lower stress, fulfillment, the lifestyle you desire, and connectivity with the people you love.

One reason businesspeople become stuck is that they have no passion for what they're doing and for whom they're doing it. Whether they have lost their passion or never had it in the first place, they all too often focus on the wrong things. They have lost track of the game they are playing, or maybe they never understood the rules to begin with. They feel impotent—unable to change their business, or their lives. Turning on and turning up the passion leads to the kind of success described above. I'll show you how.

Most people in bad times cut corners in the most treacherous way imaginable—by downsizing human or intellectual capital, the real asset of most businesses today. That is a mistake. You can find no greater upside-leveraging tools than the energy, passion, intelligence, connections, and entrepreneurial spirit of the human beings you surround yourself with. As we'll see in Chapter 10 of this book, the "I can do it myself!" mentality may work for your 6-year-old, but it doesn't work in the "sticky" business world of the twenty-first century.

Ironically, the more stuck people feel, the more attached they become to the status quo and the approaches they are currently taking, despite the lackluster results they are receiving from those efforts. But if *ever* there was an important time to test changes in the way you think about and do business right now, it's during a tough economic downturn. You might safely and conservatively test one new approach to selling, marketing, or advertising, and then discover that a second approach makes things 20 percent better. But don't stop there—the third approach might make things 40 percent better!

You could also stop at 40 percent, but why? If your industry is dropping 30 percent, you'd still be ahead—but why would you stop? You're bucking the downward trend of your industry. You're making more money, so why rest on your laurels? I've seen changes in a test approach increase business performance as much as twenty-one times—that's 2,100 percent better! And yet, most businesses that are fortunate enough to achieve an additional level of success get stuck because they settle for that incremental growth. They think better is enough—but better is never enough. As long as you're putting in the same amount of effort and time, as long as you're facing the same opportunity costs, the same prospect walking in the door could be worth 333 percent more business. So why settle for just 33 percent?

This is where all that upside leverage I've been talking about comes into play. Even in a crisis economy where your competitors are closing their doors, you can thrive. You're still growing, despite all the doom and gloom in the financial news. How does that sound?

If it sounds good, read on.

THE NINE STICKING POINTS THAT ARE GETTING IN THE WAY OF YOUR SUCCESS

This book was written to unstick your business. So to make my message more clear and digestible, I've broken it down into what I call "sticking points."

I have identified for you the nine major areas in which businesses get stuck, in good times and bad, and to each of these subjects I've devoted a chapter in this book. Every chapter will show you what the common pitfalls, traps, and missteps are at that particular sticking point. More important, I'll offer you specific solutions that you can implement *today* in your business so that you can achieve the enjoyable and even enviable growth that you deserve. I'll then show you how to have a field day capitalizing on the negative environment in the business world that exists right now. I'll show you how to implement everything you've learned.

So let's take a look at the nine sticking points. This is just an overview—you'll get specific solutions and ideas in subsequent chapters.

Some Businesses Are Stuck Losing Out to the Competition

If your competition is making gains on you, it doesn't necessarily mean they offer a better product or service. They're probably simply taking a wiser approach to positioning, marketing, and selling. It may also mean that *your* approach isn't working.

Each of these domains requires constant innovation, and yet most businesses fail to engineer a continuous flow of breakthroughs in marketing, strategy, innovation, and management.

The result? In the famous words of Peter Drucker: "Since these business owners are not constantly working to obsolesce themselves, they can rest assured that their competitors are." You can't bring about these breakthroughs unless you understand and identify what your business is doing now in each of these categories. But innovating in your business is surprisingly easy, as we'll see in Chapter 2.

In that chapter, we'll consider what it means to innovate in a business and the many wonderful ways to do it that are available to you. We'll explore the difference between *optimization* and *innovation*, and consider how few businesses engage in authentically innovative tactics. When business shifts either up or down, individuals and companies typically take one of two actions: They do either more of the same thing or less of the same thing. But their activities are *all tied to doing the same thing*, as opposed to doing something different or better, something more profitable, impactful, productive, expedient, and preemptive.

How do you engineer breakthroughs? How do you take controlled risks? How do you look outside your own industry for breakthroughs that can be applied to your business? When you've got answers to these questions, you'll no longer be stuck losing out to the competition. At the end of Chapter 2, you'll be on the path to going and growing, prospering and dominating.

Some Businesses Are Stuck Not Selling Enough

How do you change the game so that you're selling to more people, selling more things more often, and closing more sales faster and more easily? In Chapter 3, I'll introduce you to what I call the Indiana Jones School of Business—and you'll see how. It's all about changing the game, from one that cannot be won to a different game where you alone know how to win with consistency, ease, and great pleasure—in terms of both the process and the bottom-line results you achieve.

There are multiple elements of your business that can be changed for the better. First, we'll talk about how to change the way your sales force sells, which involves training all your salespeople in consultative selling techniques. Then we'll take a look at your advertising, which may be dry, tactical (rather than strategic), and ineffective. We'll talk in detail about how changing something as seemingly simple as the headlines in your advertising can bring an avalanche of new business to your doorstep.

We'll also look at changing your online presence—ever important in today's super-connected world. Do you have a website? Is it attracting the kind of business you want? If not, it's time to change it.

There are plenty of other areas in your business where change can be extremely healthy and beneficial—the way you leverage, for example, or your business's overarching message. We'll go over all of these, as well as the ways that innovation can help keep you far from deficits and cash-flow problems.

When you graduate from my Indiana Jones School of Business at the end of Chapter 3, you will have mastered preemptive selling, the unique selling proposition, the strategy of preeminence, and consultative selling—tools of the trade that will ensure you'll never be stuck not selling enough again. Change the game, change your sales strategy and tactics—and guess what? Your results will change. Very, very quickly.

Some Businesses Are Stuck with Erratic Business Volume

Erratic, unpredictable business volume occurs when a business fails to be strategic, systematic, and analytical. In Chapter 4, I'll share with you the concept of creating a successful migration strategy for advancing and enhancing relationships with buyers, as well as referrers and endorsers.

Let's define our terms. A *migration strategy* involves targeting the best quality and quantity of prospects, getting them interested in your proposition, making them a proposal they can't refuse, selling them, and continuously reselling them. You are "migrating" them into, through, and up your sales system. The strategy begins with creating an integrated system to start relationships with buyers and/or visitors to your business—including such means as the phone, your website, your catalog, your showroom technical support, product information requests, or however else they are brought into your company.

This system may include free samples, inexpensive products, complimentary education material, no-cost consults or assessments, and other means of forging a connection. It allows you to see not only who your best clients are and how to communicate with them, but also how to bring them "up and over" from the category of "just looking" (suspects) to the category of making small purchases (first-time sales), and finally to the ultimate category of making big-ticket purchases on a repeat basis (clients for life). I'll share with you approaches that have worked for the businesses I consult with—in some cases, increasing their gross by a factor of 15 in a period of just eighteen months. This outcome occurs more frequently than you might imagine—and often the best climate for it is during an economic downturn. My strategy is simply to get businesses to demand maximum performance from anything they or their teams do.

Some Businesses Are Stuck Failing to Strategize

If you were to keep a diary of all of your business activities for a month, you might discover that 80 percent of those activities are nonproductive and nonstrategic. Most entrepreneurs fail to focus on strategizing, managing, and working on higher-performing growth issues. They *micro*-manage but never *macro*-manage. They just keep on spending time, money, and human capital the way they have always spent them—with the same lackluster results. They're putting out day-to-day tactical fires—working harder and harder for the business, instead of getting the business to work harder and harder for them.

In Chapter 5, I'll help you take the term "strategy" from its lofty perch as a buzzword that everybody mentions but few entrepreneurs truly understand or implement. I'll discuss such concepts as strategy versus tactics, effectiveness and efficiency, true time management for businesspeople, and the "highest and best use" theory. I'll show you how to honestly, rapidly, and stunningly multiply your effectiveness by looking at the three to five most important and leverageable things your business is paying you to do. We'll break those tasks down into five or six subprocesses and rank them in terms of proficiency, passion, and relevance to the ongoing and future success of the business.

Some Businesses Are Stuck with Costs Eating Up All the Profits

Why do costs eat up profits for stagnating businesses?

First, most enterprises don't measure the return on their marketing investment, and even if they did, they'd find that their current marketing strategy is a sinkhole. Second, they look at cutting back the investment they make on sales and marketing during tough times, just when they need to be bolstering those functions—provided they know how to make this added investment pay off. And, third, they need to adjust their measurement horizon in terms of their overall outlook in any activity that they do, because if the business is declining, they can't operate. They need to switch to "triage" marketing, as I call it. They don't have a clue about what motivates the first-time buyer or prospect, so they're spending either too much or too little.

When the economy starts to shift downward and businesses stagnate or decline, most business owners and executives put more money into marketing *without measuring the return on investment of the marketing investment they currently have in place*. If you aren't maximizing, you're minimizing. Obviously, doing more of what wasn't working during good times won't get you through a recession! In Chapter 6, I'll show you how to analyze every activity you perform in terms of the basic, critical question: If you put $1 in, what is it that you get in return? And how much future profit do you generate? Everything you do should be measured in terms of either an investment or a profit center, as opposed to just a cost expense.

How do you shorten your company's planning and operating horizons (what the company should do for you in the short, medium, and long terms) so that you ensure not just the growth but the very survivability of your business? How do you get out of the parity pricing predicament that bedevils businesses such as fast-food chains? How do you command the extra pricing premium that a Ritz-Carlton or a Tiffany's can charge? How do you ally with bigger companies, add products from other companies, and develop access to products and technology without having to spend money and time, develop footholds in new and international markets, and have R&D performed for you for pennies on the dollar or for no cost at all? These are the types of pivotal questions I'll answer in Chapter 6.

Some Businesses Are Stuck Still Doing What's Not Working

Some entrepreneurs, business owners, and executives simply can't push themselves beyond the status quo. Most people in business, no matter what their industry, have a highly predictable tendency to transact their business from a revenue-generating stance similar to that of everyone else in the industry. But it doesn't have to be this way.

If you're doing what everybody else is doing, you aren't differentiating yourself from the competition. You're marginalizing and commoditizing yourself. In Chapter 7, we'll talk about how you can stop doing what's not working, avoid status quo thinking, and get into the habit of testing, measuring, and examining higher- and better-performing options, activities, and approaches. I'll prepare you to move forward with new, effective breakthrough solutions. These solutions, though potentially driving forces, may be completely unused in your field right now.

Some Businesses Are Stuck Being Marginalized by the Marketplace

The starting point for success is your own vision and image of yourself and your business. If you think you're a commodity, a generic product, or a service like any other, then that's what you'll be. It's a self-fulfilling prophecy. You'll do what everyone else does: You'll price the same way as everyone else, and you'll sell, market, communicate, deal with people, and relate to clients the same way as everyone else. That's akin to accepting your own death sentence.

If you sell the same thing at the same price and in the same way as everyone else, you must add value, or you will be marginalized by the marketplace. Value can take the form of more bonuses, more benefits, a better guarantee, more access, or more technical support. You've got to distinguish yourself, your product, your company, and your business model in ways that make you unlike anyone else—and, more specifically, in ways that associate you with highly distinctive and desirable value. If you do that, you will stand out favorably, and you'll have removed yourself from the world of commoditized companies.

In Chapter 8, I'll show you how to be seen as preeminent, preemptive, and proprietary. Every human being—including every prospect and buyer, and certainly every businessperson—has a perpetual need to feel special. Well, the same is true of businesses: They need to appear special in the marketplace, or they risk being swept away, marginalized, and turned into commodities. Meeting this challenge involves making your buyers feel special, valued, and respected. I'll show you how.

Some Businesses Are Stuck with Mediocre Marketing

Most entrepreneurs fail to understand that the difference between mediocrity and making millions has more to do with effective marketing than with any other single factor. In Chapter 9, we'll talk about what can happen when you learn to capitalize on marketing's geometric capability to explode your business upward. My definition of marketing is simple: It's all about "teaching" the folks in a given marketplace that your particular business can solve their problems, fill their voids, or achieve opportunities, hopes, and goals the way no other business can. Your consumers and prospects may never even have verbalized these problems. Yet if your business can get the chance to powerfully communicate about its ability to do these things, it *will* experience outstanding growth.

Marketing is the bedrock of virtually every enduring dominant business in every field. You must be a superior marketer. The good news is that great marketers are made, not born. Learning how to market efficiently, powerfully, and profitably is a simple and surprisingly logical process, despite all the complexity that many authors and so-called experts have brought to the table.

If you're willing to shoot for the moon and the stars and trust me to guide you, we'll get there. In Chapter 9, you'll find out how to achieve a true 20/20 vision and a laser-like cutting-edge focus in marketing that will make your business skyrocket. Our emphasis in that chapter is on what you'll do, not just on what you'll understand.

Some Businesses Are Stuck Saying "I Can Do It Myself!"

It's appropriate for a child to say, "I can do it myself!" When tying their shoes, buckling a seat belt, or shooting a basket, children need to be encouraged to learn to fend for themselves. But in the business world, the notion of "I can do it myself!" leads far more often to heartache and failure than to success.

In Chapter 10, I'll show you how to create enormous new vistas of wealth and success for yourself and your business by letting go of the childlike mantra "I can do it myself!" This belief severely limits what you can do; it also limits your knowledge base, your skill level, and your earnings. You may think you can't afford to delegate. But in fact, you can't afford *not* to.

What can you do through other people that you can't do by yourself? At heart, entrepreneurism is all about leveraging people, skill sets, assets, capital, and efforts. In Chapter 10, I'll teach you the art of leveraging the talents of others in such a way that your collaborative efforts will dwarf any success you might have achieved on your own, no matter how talented you may be. I'll show you how to create your own board of advisors—what Napoleon Hill called the "Mastermind Group." I'll show you how to take advantage of OPE (other people's efforts), OPI (other people's ideas), OPS/K (other people's skill and knowledge), and OPRR (other people's resources and relationships). As a result, more of what used to be OPM—other people's money—will be *your* money.

TODAY'S JOURNEY TOWARD AN UNSTUCK TOMORROW

What's it like to be unstuck? What's it like to be no longer plagued by the nine variations on the theme of stuckness that this book will confront?

To answer that question, think about the most exhilarating experiences of your life—your wedding day, the days on which your children were born, the touchdown you scored for your high school or college team. That's the level of excitement, joy, and exhilaration you can experience *every working day*. This sounds like a huge promise, so let me show you why I say that.

First, you'll be in total control of your destiny. You'll avoid being snuffed out by a negative economy or by your competition. You'll be ignited, because hard times are only more reason for you to soar above everyone else. You'll know with predictability what tomorrow will bring. Your business will be working harder for you than you're working for it. You'll have multiple activities strategically performing for you by sourcing new revenue, new buyers, and new prospects and migrating them through a systematic, sequential process forever. You'll have systems in place, where applicable, that will bring in innumerable high-quality referrals as well as the highest purchasing and most profitable people your business could have. And, finally, you'll be building your business in such a way that it becomes a prized asset sellable by anyone in the world, because it's got systems in place, processes, predictability, profitability, and sustainability.

The iconic model of the entrepreneur in the twentieth century was the self-made man or woman going it alone. But success in the twenty-first-century business environment requires the ability to collaborate creatively with others. No one can know everything or have every single piece of the puzzle. Continuing to think that such things are possible is selfish, for three reasons. First, if you have a great product, service, or company, you've earned the right to be a contributor to your marketplace, and your success will only be a by-product of that contribution. Second, whether you are an entrepreneur or a corporate executive, your family is looking to you to make your business and your career as fulfilling, unstressful, and asset-accruing and -enriching as it can be for you and them. And, third, you owe it to your employees, investors, and other stakeholders to make your business as profitable, sustainable, and desirable a choice in the consumer's mind as it can be.

Getting unstuck is about choosing the fastest and easiest ways to make a difference, so that you create more wins for yourself. Doing so will animate your spirit, your sense of possibility—and your treasury!

It is the certainty of knowing you have a systematic approach in place that is continuously attracting new people (whether prospects or buyers, depending on your business model), and turning them from first-time buyers into ongoing, recurring clients and clients for life, that allows you to constantly improve and expand your revenue and business model. You are operating out of your passion to an exponential degree. You are getting the most upside leverage performance and connectivity, now and in the future, out of everything you are doing. You are totally strategic. You know the exact impact, cost, and cause and effect of everything you are doing. You are well-hedged because you have multiple sources of income. You have built a massively strong edifice with an impervious and impenetrable foundation. You are constantly counter-programming everyone else, so that you are distinctive and differentiated. Within your niche market, you are seen as the only viable solution. You understand and articulate the market's needs, hopes, dreams, and problems better than anyone else, and you offer clear-cut solutions that your market will prize and desire exclusively from you. You are in total control of what you are doing and where you are going. You have a specific plan of action you can diligently follow, master, and adjust—and you have an exit strategy, whether this entails selling the business, turning it over to the employees, or anything else. You have moved from uncertainty to absolute certainty, from confusion to exhilarating joy.

Remember the Tin Man in *The Wizard of Oz*? A little bit of oil, applied judiciously in the right places, got him moving again. He didn't have to go back to the shop in order to continue traveling down the yellow brick road—he just needed those few drops of oil, applied with care exactly where they were needed.

That's what this book is about—showing you how to go, how to grow, and how to maximize the enjoyment and profitability of the business upon which you have already lavished so much time, care, and attention.

Each chapter offers dozens of proven ideas about how to get unstuck, and I candidly acknowledge that the wealth of concepts I'll share with you can prove overwhelming. So in addition to chapter summaries reiterating the key points I've made, I'll conclude each subsequent chapter with a specific action step to be taken *right now*—what I call an "Immediate Action Step."

Ready for the nine sticking points?

Prepare yourself to be unstuck.

2

ARE YOU STUCK LOSING OUT TO THE COMPETITION?

There's no denying it: It's a dog-eat-dog world. And the business world is no different—if anything, the canines there might be even *more* cannibalistic. So how do you come out on top? How do you ensure that your products and services beat out all the rest?

Peter Drucker—in my opinion, the greatest business thinker of the twentieth century—once said, "Marketing and innovation produce results; all the rest are costs." I would add a third income-generating activity to his statement: strategizing.

And yet, despite the fact that marketing, innovation, and strategizing tower above anything else businesspeople could be doing for their businesses, most of them fail to engineer a continuous flow of breakthroughs in these three key areas. As a result, although they are not obsolescing themselves, they can rest assured that their competitors are.

If you're losing out to the competition, it's time to do something different. In this chapter, you'll learn how to launch your business forward so that your competitors are left standing in the dust, wondering what the hell happened. All it takes is a little innovation and a killer strategy. In other words, a different approach. Let's look at an example.

A few years ago, I had two friends who each discovered the same business opportunity but approached it in radically different ways—one tactical and shortsighted, the other strategic and focused on the long term.

The first, Tom, was a gifted copywriter who saw potential in the over-looked market of simulated diamonds, or cubic zirconium. For $30,000, he ran a full-page ad in the *Los Angeles Times* announcing his new enterprise, the Beverly Hills Diamond Company, and its key product, a loose, one-karat stone that sold for $39. The wonderfully crafted ad pulled in about $42,000 worth of sales, which amounted to about $3,000 profit after all expenses. Tom, who was used to making massive, front-end profits, didn't see enough profit in the concept, so he folded his tent and left.

The second friend, Larry, didn't possess Tom's copywriting prowess, but he was a world-class strategist—and strategy will always trump copy. Larry soldiered into the very same marketplace, armed with a game plan for an identical product but a very different result. His ad wasn't as well written, and so Van Pliss and Tissany (his take on Van Cleef & Arpel and Tiffany, which were hot brands at the time) pulled in only $28,000 from his $30,000 ad—meaning he'd lost $2,000 before he'd even counted overhead.

But instead of getting frustrated, Larry continued with the next phase of his strategy. Whereas Tom had mailed his product in a chintzy cardboard box, Larry delivered his in a high-end jeweler's case, which in turn was placed in a velvet bag—packaging that cost a pretty penny beyond what he'd already spent on the ad. Along with that, Larry included a letter:

> Thank you for purchasing your Van Pliss and Tissany one-karat gemstone. When you remove it from its beautiful jeweler's case, you'll immediately notice its fiery brilliance, which is even more beautiful than we promised.
>
> You may also notice that the stone is smaller than you expected—but that's the nature of the Van Pliss diamond. In order to achieve such extraordinary brilliance, our gem is denser, which makes it 25 percent smaller than most people expect. However, the brilliance of the diamond inspires many of our buyers to upgrade to larger five- and ten-karat stones, which they hope to then set. Be-

cause we've experienced this so often, we've set some of our most magnificent five- and ten-karat stones in fourteen- and eighteen-k rings, necklaces, earrings, and bracelets, which you can find in the accompanying catalog. And, more important, because we do such volume, we have manufactured these jewelry pieces ourselves, thus slashing the price by 50 percent of what you would pay for the same product from a jewelry store.

We would like to offer you the chance to upgrade: Not only have we included a pre-paid return carton and UPS form, but we are also extending you double credit. In addition, any purchase you make with us will not be considered binding on your part until you've had the set jewelry item in your possession for thirty days. If your family and friends don't remark on how beautiful your new gem is, or if you find that buying the same piece from a jeweler would have saved you money, you may return your gemstone and setting, no questions asked.

What was the end difference between Tom's tactics and Larry's strategy? Whereas Tom made $3,000 and promptly quit, Larry's strategy lost $2,000 up front, then netted him $25 million in his first year of business alone.

That's the difference.

If you come up with a killer strategy and a dynamite approach, you can make a killing, too.

OPTIMIZATION VERSUS INNOVATION: YOU NEED BOTH TO BRING YOUR BUSINESS TO A WHOLE NEW LEVEL

Believe it or not, a very high percentage of businesspeople are Toms, not Larrys. Most businesspeople never take a deep breath and ask themselves this question: Is the approach I'm using to generate and sustain business anywhere close to the highest and best approach out there?

The reason Larry made $25 million while Tom made only a few grand is simple: Larry's innovative strategy allowed him to stand out from the competition. When it came to marketing and selling the gemstone, Larry had the guts to think outside the jewelry box.

A lot of people confuse innovation with optimization, two popular buzzwords in business today. But each is a distinct concept. *Optimization* means taking an existing process and making it work to its optimum, where it generates the most income for the least amount of investment—whether that investment is in time, risk, or capital. To optimize, you first have to know how activities involved in your revenue system are performing. If an activity isn't performing, you have to replace it or improve it. If it is performing, you have to maximize that performance. That's optimization: taking what's working and making it work to the *n*th degree; or fixing or replacing what's not working.

Innovation, by contrast, is a messy, unpredictable proposition. A business must engineer breakthroughs, take controlled risks, and look outside the industry for new ideas. When approached correctly, innovation is gutsy and exciting, and will put a world of opportunity at your feet. I'll teach you how to turn innovation into something more than just a buzzword or wistful hope.

Optimization and innovation are both crucial to your success, but the order is important. For just a little while, let's go through Jay Abraham 101. If you called me in to work on your business, I'd start by breaking down my activities into two stages: optimization followed by innovation. Here's how I'd do it.

In Stage 1 (optimization), I'd work on making the activities you're currently performing even better—not because they necessarily represent the best and highest use, but because you don't want to jeopardize your current business in your search for higher-performing alternatives. Every current revenue-generating activity would undergo optimization until it became stabilized, at which point we'd enter Stage 2: innovation.

Here's where we would use the increased funding generated by the optimization in Stage 1 to research new approaches to replace and sometimes complement less effective activities. Innovation basically involves making obsolete that which you did before.

At their core, innovation and optimization rest on fundamentally different principles. But integrating the two will bring your business to a whole new level.

RECOGNIZING THE SIGNS OF WHAT'S WORKING AND WHAT'S NOT

As I pointed out in Chapter 1, when business shifts either up or down, companies do one of two things: either more of the same thing or less of the same thing. One way or another, their activities are all tied to doing the same thing, as opposed to doing something different or doing different combinations of things. Here's where innovation comes in.

The key is being able to recognize the following:

- What you're doing isn't the only way you could be doing it.

- If you start doing something different, you must compare it to what you were previously doing in order to best judge its impact.

- If you discover a better approach, it's time to scale up; if not, it's time to move on to something else.

Over the last thirty years, I've had the good fortune to see who has emerged successfully—through good times and bad—in many different industries. Without fail, the leaders of the pack are always those who engineer the maximum quantity, quality, and consistency in breakthroughs, whether in marketing, strategy, innovation, or management.

I've dedicated my life to finding the highest-performing and safest ways to maximize business activities and performance—what I like to call the "good kind of leverage." It's kind of like the two different kinds of cholesterol, one of which will clog your arteries and kill you, and the other, which can counteract the bad.

Same goes for leverage. Bad leverage has brought ruination to the mortgage field, which is crumbling to its foundation even as I write this book. You'll also see bad leverage when a business invests in an asset—equipment, employees, or other overhead—that increases its long-term, fixed obligation with no certainty that the investment will produce a return exceeding its cost, let alone appreciate. That's quite a risk. Sure, if it works out, you're in the clear. But if it doesn't—well, let's just say that you could end up losing more than your derriere.

I don't deal in dangerous leverage. I deal in new approaches that dramatically multiply results—but I work with a net, one really big safety net that makes risk practically nonexistent. I look for changes that improve your results the moment you implement them. Innovation has no value unless it brings a greater and more perceptible advantage to the marketplace—an advantage that hopefully comes exclusively from you.

THE POWER OF MARKETING—WHICH MOST PEOPLE IGNORE

So what kind of innovative strategies will help you achieve good leverage? And how do you use this leverage to jump ahead of your competitors in the marketplace? The answer is actually right in front of you, a part of the word "market-place" itself: *marketing*.

Most small- and medium-sized company owners don't market *at all*. And the few who do—well, they tend to market very traditionally, which is a euphemistic way of saying "ineffectually." They neither monitor performance nor strive to improve marketing variables that could give them this geometric boost. (Marketing variables are factors that can cause huge swings in results.) They generally aren't even aware that their marketing has that kind of capability. It's as if they'd purchased a twelve-cylinder Jaguar, but only six cylinders are firing: They have enough power to drive, but if they just cleaned out the clog and applied some lube, they could have twice the power far more efficiently and economically.

When you change your marketing, you change your results. Even small changes add up. I've seen minor changes to advertisements—rewording the business proposition, say, or removing the client's perceived risk in a transaction—yield as much as a 21 percent improvement. For instance, instead of saying just "Buy my widget," I changed a client's message to "Buy my widget *now* because. . . ." The result was not only a 30 to 40 percent sales increase but an *immediate* one.

That's just one application. I've seen sales quadruple as a consequence of changes in the medium by which business owners reach the marketplace. I've seen a simple tweak in copy on a tradeshow sign triple the traffic and quadruple the *quality* of the traffic, meaning the ultimate profitability of the prospects. I've seen a single follow-up effort after an unsuccessful sales call bring 35 percent of prospects back to buy. I've seen other follow-up calls produce 50 percent more sales with previous clients. Bottom line: Change your marketing, change your results.

Most owners of small-to medium-sized businesses don't have a clue as to how many leverage points are available to them. In every business, there are many areas in any given revenue-generating activity. Let's say you own a company that's just placed an ad in the Yellow Pages. One leverage point could be as simple as changing the body copy (meaning the words that follow the headline). You could also change the placement of the ad on the page (going from horizontal to vertical or from left to right). And, finally, you could shift the location of each of the ad elements within the ad itself. That's three leverage points right there—and you've racked them up even before getting to the call from the client!

Ads are designed to generate calls, visits, and e-mails, and there are multiple leverage points to be found once you reach the call response stage. What you say or do at the point of contact can increase the odds of a purchase by as much as 75 percent.

Marketing is further discussed in Chapters 8 and 9, but right now I'll share with you fifteen points that I developed with my friend and partner, the brilliant Internet marketer Rich Schefren.* These points are personality building blocks that will help you position yourself, your company, and/or your product as a preeminent persona in your marketplace—poised to stand head and shoulders above the competition. Think of them as grist for the mill.

Fifteen Ways to Position Yourself, Your Product, or Your Company as Preeminent in Your Marketplace

1. Attach the suffix "In your service" to everything you do for your clients. You are their trusted advisor for life.

2. Don't be afraid to say what your competition won't. In any transaction, tell your client, "Here's what you're not being told."

3. Don't hesitate to extol your own achievements and value—but do it in the context of the benefit it brings to the client. Practice

---

*I drew heavily from Rick's material in the writing of this book, and I want to acknowledge him for the original research he performed, the outstanding analysis he developed, and the writing that developed from all of his hard work.

at it, do it with humility and humanity, and make it heartfelt and graceful, not overbearing.

4. List your flaws. Your clients are human, and so are you. So acknowledge it. Doing so makes you real and honest in their eyes.

5. Cultivate the habit of looking at each relationship as a long-term investment you're making in the marketplace. It's not a one-night stand. It's a total attitude shift.

6. Know your strengths and weaknesses, and play to the former. The task is simple, but most people don't do it; they get caught up trying to improve their weaknesses. No leverage there.

7. Control your risk. But always point out the overlooked risks and dangers your marketplace is exposed to, and help your clients reduce or eliminate them.

8. Use as much research and data as you can to make your point, prove your advantage, and demonstrate your performance. Just be sure to summarize, compare, interpret, and analyze this information so that people can appreciate and act on it.

9. Challenge status quo thinking with a sharper, fresher perspective, a better strategy, or a clearer game plan for your market to follow.

10. Continually add to your brand equity by doing more, caring more, contributing more.

11. Form alliances and advisory boards. (We'll talk about nurturing strategic relationships in Chapter 10.)

12. Use endorsements and testimonials properly and often. You can garner these from buyers, community influences, and press articles.

13. Hire the best. Pay them richly. But pay them mostly on performance.

14. If you're invisible, you can't become the go-to source. Make yourself, your product, or your company known. Do it impactfully. Do it with the right people. Make the impact worth the effort.

15. Learn to project the image of true success—long before you've fully achieved it. It's only a matter of time before it will occur.

These fifteen points serve as the ideal reminder that you have to view changes in the granular sense. "Change"—that all-encompassing, poetic, sweeping notion—is not going to cut it. You need tangible, actionable steps to follow. So instead of focusing on change, focus on *changes*.

An added benefit of changes (in the plural) is that they will increase your business's success with speed and efficacy. As an analogy, let's say you decide to improve the performance of your car by adding a turbo charger and changing the wheels, which you assume will give you more power and more speed, respectively. In actuality, however, the combined benefit of both improvements would be exponential, because faster tires combined with more power equals even *more* speed. Implementing multiple enhancements is how I've helped businesses achieve such great results so rapidly.

ASKING THE RIGHT QUESTIONS ABOUT HOW TO MAKE YOUR BUSINESS MORE SUCCESSFUL

After reading the previous list, you may be thinking, "Whoa, fifteen actionable points is a lot. Where do I begin?" Well, the truth is, even if you did only three of those things, or two, or even *just one*, you'd still be leaps and bounds beyond your competitors. Why? Because most people aren't asking the right questions.

Instead of projecting ahead and thinking of ways to change the way they do things, most businesspeople are consumed with self-doubt. They're struggling with the wrong questions. They continually ask themselves, "Am I worthy of this business?" That translates into many more complicated questions, such as the following:

- "Can I really sustain this business?"

- "Can I compete with all these bigger competitors?"

- "Can I really make enough money to retire in comfort, put my kids through college, and take a two-week vacation each year?"

- "Can I really keep this business viable?"

Don't ask, "Am I worthy of this business?" Instead you should be asking yourself if this business is worthy of *you*.

I'm going to give you the answer to the first question right now: You are. So start acting like it!

Once you realize how much more is possible from your time and efforts, you'll see that your business is the greatest wealth-creating vehicle you'll ever have. Why not give it all you've got?

For starters, that means marketing. Marketing is the key to launching your business far beyond the status quo of the average Joe. Don't fall into the trap of thinking of marketing as an expenditure. Marketing is an *investment*. With the right marketing, you can increase the profit of your business by as much as 200 percent every year. And anytime you increase profit, you're increasing your business's value at least five times that.

In order to increase your profit, you need to remember this mantra:

Change your strategy, change your results.

Unfortunately, most owners of small- to medium-sized businesses have no strategy at all. They're tactical, rather than strategic. All they do is struggle through the end of the month, only to start over again at the top of the next calendar page, hoping they'll make it through again. They're like Tom from the story at the beginning of this chapter: only looking at the here and now, and missing out on all the long-term potential.

As an entrepreneur, you *need* a long-term strategy that drives every activity in your business—from tracking prospects, to closing the sale, to reselling them something worthwhile again and again. All your activities should be designed to deploy, maintain, and advance that strategy. Success doesn't come from saying "I have to make money this week." It comes from having, knowing, and following your long-term, end-game strategy.

If you're a dentist, for example, your strategy might be "We're going to source prospects from the dental industry and migrate them through a pipeline that keeps reselling at a higher quantity and thus a higher revenue level. From there, we'll induce referrals, consciously and systematically. We know exactly what the progression steps and actions will be, and we're going to control them proactively. Everything we do will drive that systematic, progressive outcome." *That's* being strategic.

Most businesspeople don't realize that strategy is all-important. As Stephen Covey put it in his bestselling book *The 7 Habits of Highly Effective People*, "Begin with the end in mind." Being without a strategy is like deciding to build a house with no idea about how many bathrooms it will have or where you'll put the kitchen. You can't just bang some nails into wood and hope the outcome resembles a habitable dwelling. But that's similar to what businesses do every day. Let's look at another real-world example.

Many years ago, one of my clients was a brokerage firm that sold gold and silver. The owners were very tactical, bringing in clients episodically, selling them once, and then seeking new ones. I eliminated that static thinking and replaced it with a master strategy.

In the first stage, we sought the most qualified prospects in the most consistent and cost-effective way possible. We led them through a process in which we educated them about the product, and then sold them a modest amount of the safest and most appealing initial investment. We wanted our clients to be comfortable, which we told them going in. That builds trust.

Then, we moved them to a second transaction of greater quantity and quality, as part of the next step in our long-term relationship. Based on the strategy underlying this relationship, we started them with gold, then moved them to silver, then rare coins, then gold stocks, and then other collectibles if they were appropriate. We had a systematic approach. Our first stage was not designed to hit and run. It was designed to sell and set up an ethical process for a sequential, long-term relationship future.

As another part of this stage, we accessed every newsletter out there. We offered investment seminars. This was at a time before Krugerrands had been outlawed, and the minter of the Krugerrands was brimming with wealth. We saw an opportunity and leveraged it, getting the Krugerrand minter to pay 100 percent of our advertising costs in the *Wall Street Journal* and all our marketing costs for millions of pieces of direct mail. At any one time, we had in motion no fewer than twenty different activities—all nontraditional methods of credibly and impactfully reaching the most desirable category of buyer.

Once our strategy was under way, there was no stopping us. While our next-closest competitor was pulling in $50 million in revenues, we were doing $500 million. Strategy was the key to winning the race, ten times over.

THE STRATEGY OF PREEMINENCE: MAKE YOURSELF KNOWN

Do you honestly believe that Dr. Phil is the best, most highly trained psychologist in America? He may not be the best, but he is certainly the best paid—earning 20, 50, even 100 times more than others in his field. But the difference between Dr. Phil and the average neighborhood shrink has nothing to do with his knowledge or credentials. It has to do with his positioning, his superior personal branding, and his willingness to tell his own story. In short: It comes from his *visibility in the marketplace*. There are literally thousands of ordinary businesspeople, once virtual "nobodies" in their markets, who have become preeminent and now enjoy success far beyond anything they could have imagined possible. The good news is: Preeminent businesspeople are *made*, not born.

An important part of beating out your competition is employing a strategy of preeminence, which means making your business resonate at a perceived higher value in the mind of your market. You want to stand out and above the rest of the marketplace by creating an aura of superiority that decisively differentiates your brand from all the other run-of-the-mill competitors. Superiority, however, is critically different from arrogance. Look at the most prized and valued advisors in any field. They're usually the highest paid and the most sought after, because they rank quantum times higher in terms of the respect they inspire.

Let's use my own business as an example. I've established myself as an authoritative marketing consultant, one who can command well above the standard industry rate. Part of this perception on the part of the client is psychological, and I make certain that this view is maintained by differentiating my relationship, conduct, and ongoing level of contribution from that of my competitors. I have control of the relationship, and that comes with the certainty of knowing what I'm steering that relationship toward. Most people have no control over their selling relationships, and so they're forced to be reactive.

The first step you have to take is to view your business as the market's most trusted, valued, and prized provider, advisor, and source. Your perception and persona immediately transform the relationship with the client. From today forward, you have to change the way you view and run your business and interact with your clients so that you see yourself as their most trusted confidante in your field, the definitive expert source, the true market "maven."

At the heart of it all, you also have to believe that what you're doing is for a greater good, that you're truly being selfless in your business goal to serve the prospects/clients better and more fully than any other competitor does. Sure, you're getting paid in return (it's the reward for doing more for them), but that's nothing compared to the quality of service you're providing your clients, who become your business's center of attention. Your goal cannot be to get rich. Your goal must be to make the clients' life or business richer, more protected, and more fulfilled so that they get more out of the process of doing business, or out of life itself.

A colleague of mine and an internationally admired expert in sales training, Chet Holmes, came up with an ingenious and powerfully effective method for establishing business preeminence: Simply tell the consumer what the buying criteria should be for purchasing products or services from your own marketplace. Then make absolutely certain that your company's product or service is the only one that fully and consistently satisfies (or *over*-satisfies) those criteria.

Many famous brands have employed this tactic. Think of Dr. Pepper's "23 Flavors" campaign. Before you knew that Dr. Pepper used a blend of twenty-three flavors to create its distinctive taste, did it matter to you how many chemicals were involved? Is a beverage with only one flavor something you wouldn't have considered drinking? Probably not. In fact, many other beverage companies also use a blend of flavors in the double-digits, but when the Dr. Pepper commercials and packaging began emphasizing "23 Flavors," what they were implying was that other flavoring methods were inferior. Dr. Pepper's beverage alone met the criterion of being prepared in the most creative manner possible—as defined by Dr. Pepper.

If you can't be the *only* business to satisfy certain criteria, then be the first to tell the marketplace what those criteria are and that you satisfy them, before your competitors do. Advertise what you do, how you do it, why you do it, and what doing it means to the betterment of the buyer. In preemptive marketing, a company details the business process—from the moment the idea was born to the delivery of the product to the consumer's doorstep—as a means of setting it dimensionally and incomparably apart from the competition, even if the process is identical to that of its competitors. By being the first to publicly define, describe, and revere the process, your business gains full credit. Everyone else looks like a clone, and you achieve proprietary preeminence and preemptive status. Here's another example.

Years ago, I represented a high-end women's clothier and shoe store that netted several million dollars annually. To justify the $500 price tag on a pair of stilettos, we made a point of explaining how those shoes were different. We explained how the manufacturer scrutinized more than 100 skins to find a single matching set. Dyes were five times more expensive than standard market rate. The grade of silk threads was so lustrous that they cost ten times more than other shoes.

But that's how all expensive shoes are made. The difference was that we were the only ones to reveal and revere this procedure (then explain and teach it to the consumer), and that made us more distinctive and desirable—indeed, preeminent in our clients' eyes.

I then went a step further. I described the process the store's buyers went through to source the merchandise in the stores. I got out the word that they traveled 500,000 miles every year, with multiple flights to Europe, Asia, and North America (especially Chicago and New York). In the process, the buying team walked up and down a combined 10,000 flights of stairs, and reviewed, interviewed, and painstakingly evaluated 80,000 different vendors in order to choose the mere 112 unique and distinctive items that would eventually make it to their stores.

The numbers were impressive, even though virtually any clothier could have tallied the same sums. But we stood out, predominantly and preemptively, because nobody else had ever laid out the details for the client.

We've barely scraped the surface of preeminence, so we'll explore it in more depth in Chapter 8. For now, though, start brainstorming ways to position yourself as the preeminent provider of your product or services in your corner of the marketplace. You won't be sorry you did.

DON'T BE JUST A SHEEP

Most entrepreneurs are sheep. They run business by applying whatever actions they've observed in the industry—not because it's the optimal way but because that's all they know. As an example, consider this story.

A few years ago, I had a client who was in the software business, with a company that was losing out on a lot of business to a competitor. The other company had better salespeople, but its software was full of bugs. Still, the other company was getting all the business. So the first company came to me and explained its problem. "We know our software is superior," the owners told me, "but we're obviously doing something wrong. What should we do differently?"

I love hearing that question. As soon as you open your mind to doing things differently, the doors of opportunity practically fly off their hinges. I worked with these guys to develop a long-term strategy whereby we went to people who had bought the inferior software from the other company, and we gave them full credit for what they'd already paid. We awarded that credit for the other company's software *against ours* if they wanted to trade in and even advanced the cost of converting over. The response was huge: People saw that we were strategically long term. The company won back all kinds of business as a result, and the competition was left wondering what hit them.

In a rough economy, it's more important than ever to play good defense. You can't afford to lose valuable business to your competitors. But here's the good news: All you have to do to regain your competitive edge is to get creative about doing things differently—just as Larry did when he packaged cubic zirconium in a lavish velvet bag, accompanied by an elegant letter. Of course, people tend not to be very good at imagining an alternative course of action when they're high on the hog, but this is exactly why I say today's bad economy has a silver lining: It's a wonderful opportunity to shift your thinking.

It may sound unbelievable, but over the years I've had the good fortune of serving clients in 465 different industries, either directly or through consulting work; worked with or spoken to over 500,000 businesspeople in group settings; and guided more than 300 industry leaders and increased the fortunes of over 1,000 private clients. Throughout my career, I have kept careful track of each project and contact, so that I can learn from each one. This means I've seen more business strategies in action, whether delightfully successful or desperately unavailing, than just about any other human being on the planet.

Unfortunately, many businesspeople have spent the majority of their careers in the cocoon or bell jar of their own industry, never seeing the wealth of more powerful, profitable ideas swirling in the economy around them. I'd like to be more than just a breath of fresh air—more like a torrent of cleansing clarity!

In all probability, what you've been doing has been marginal at best and, at worst, detrimental. So change it. Pull yourself out of the sheep pen—you're not going to get anywhere with the wool over your eyes. Optimize and fix what isn't working. Innovate and try new things. Develop a long-term strategy. Begin a passionate love affair with marketing. And always remember: Your business is worth it. The moment is yours.

Now it's time to introduce you to that little-known guru of the business world: Indiana Jones.

The Bottom Line

- Marketing, innovation, and strategizing produce results; all the rest are costs.

- Stage 1, finding the highest and best use, is *optimization*: taking what's working and making it work to the nth degree; or, fixing or replacing what's not working.

- Stage 2 is *innovation*: engineering breakthroughs, taking controlled risks, and looking outside the industry for new ideas.

- Instead of focusing on change, focus on *changes.*

- Ask the right questions: not "Am I worthy of this goal?" but "Is this goal worthy of *me*?"

- View your business as the market's most trusted, valued, and prized provider, advisor, and source: What you do is for a greater good, and you're truly being selfless in your business goal to serve the client better and more fully than any other competitor does.

Change your strategy, change your results.

☞ **Immediate Action Step** After reviewing the list of "Fifteen Ways to Position Yourself, Your Product, or Your Company as Preeminent in Your Marketplace," choose one thing on that list—and do it *now.*

3

ARE YOU STUCK NOT SELLING ENOUGH?

Remember the original *Raiders of the Lost Ark*? If you do, you'll no doubt recall the following scene.

Indiana Jones, our hero, is being chased through an Egyptian bazaar by a bunch of scary-looking bad guys in turbans. Trying to escape, he slips down a side street that turns out to be a blind alley. He gets to the end of the alley and there's a seven-foot-tall giant, spinning two massive Moroccan scimitars. For one tense moment, the audience thinks that Indiana is a goner.

Until Indy draws his gun and shoots him.

Now *that's* what I call changing the game.

When it comes to being stuck not selling enough, it's all about changing the game. I call this the Indiana Jones School of Business. In this chapter, I'll teach you how to shoot with guns instead of hopelessly defending yourself from seven-foot giants wielding knives.

At least metaphorically speaking. When it comes to real-life duels with swashbuckling cretins, you're on your own.

Indy's tactic is precisely the concept that needs to be employed in business: *You can change the game you play in an instant.* Most people are stuck not selling enough because they don't know how to sell products or services effectively. But there are a lot of ways to sell effectively! Depending on what you sell (whether it's a product or a service), to whom you sell it, and how you currently sell it, you must evaluate whether or not yours is the most efficient and productive way to reach, motivate, and persuade the market to buy from you, the first time and then each time thereafter. When it comes to selling more, change is the name of the game. Or, rather, *changes*.

While your competitors are stuck fighting each other with swords, you can blast them all away with some basic changes to the most important aspects of any twenty-first-century business.

Who knew that a professor of archaeology with a penchant for adventure could teach us a thing or two about business, too?

CHANGE THE WAY YOUR SALES FORCE SELLS

Let's start with the most obvious point: If you're stuck not selling enough, change the way your sales force sells. Whether you sell computer software or own a lumber company, whether you head up a marketing firm or a temp agency, your salespeople are responsible for selling your product or service—and selling it well.

Most businesses follow the basic model of maintaining a sales team. This team can be onsite or off, working via phone or in person; it can even be a third party, made up of distributors, manufacturers, and reps.

If you use salespeople of any sort—and chances are you do—the first thing you have to do is *get them trained in consultative selling*. Most people's idea of training salespeople is to introduce them to the territory and the product catalogue. I've got news for you: That's not sales training.

Consultative selling, also known as consultative advisory selling, takes sales to the next level—and beyond. It emphasizes client needs and how your product or service can not only meet those needs but actually provide *more value* to the client than just the face value of what they purchased. With this dynamic method, your salespeople are no longer pushing a product or service that may or may not meet the client's need; instead, they are working as consultants who first determine the client's need, *then* provide the solution. Suddenly, in the client's mind, you're no longer just another business like all the rest—you're the most trusted advisor.

The difference between consultative sales training and old-school technique-driven sales training is like that between night and day. With the simple shift to consultative sales, you can triple, quadruple, or even quintuple your sales. No matter what form your sales force takes—whether onsite handling walk-ins or offsite making cold calls, whether salaried or working on commission—your first step is to get your sales team trained in consultative selling.

But don't stop there. Every other team member who has public contact must be trained in consultative sales, too. This includes your receptionist, your service people, your client service representatives, your employees in accounts receivable—and the list goes on. The fact is that they are all strategic extensions of your business's voice, determining the positioning and preeminence you create for yourself in the public eye of your marketplace.

You might be worried that training a consultative sales force will be a drain on your resources, but—as all of my clients have been surprised to discover—the actual expense is modest. In fact, it's far less than the typical profit increase your new sales approach can stimulate in only the first month or two during which you apply it. It rarely costs more than a few hundred dollars, at most a few thousand, and that one-time investment can translate into hundreds of thousands—even millions—of dollars more for your business.

Remember: Your salespeople are the first line of offense. Having salespeople and contact staff untrained in consultative sales is like running an airline with pilots who've never cracked open a flight manual.

A lot of businesspeople get intimidated by sales because they believe it's an art form, something intangible, and a person either "has it" or doesn't. Lucky for us, they're wrong. Consultative sales is a science, and it can be systematically learned and implemented by anyone. Also, it's based on a fundamental, human emotion we all possess: empathy.

Although I've seen its astronomical rates of success again and again in every imaginable industry, I don't consider myself an expert in consultative sales. So, what follows is a paraphrasing of the advice of my good friend Andy Miller, who has one of the most brilliant sales minds in business. When Andy was 27, he bought the rights to a Dutch software company, grew it to $24 million, and sold it. He has sat on the advisory boards of four different groups, which gave him access to universities that teach sales in the United States—a subject that wasn't taught at all until only fifteen years ago.

People who teach sales have to research it, and since sales has become part of university curricula, we're beginning to find out what's truth and what's myth. Through his university network, Andy has access to all of this research and has developed his approach accordingly. If you take his system to heart and act on his simple instructions, you'll very quickly see that the concept of consultative sales is a whole new ballgame, dramatically different from the old one—and dramatically more effective.

Consultative advisory sales can be applied to any business in any industry in any country. It fits no matter where you are. You'll find, however, that two aspects will vary, depending on your country and culture:

- How you build relationships

- How you make decisions

In some cultures, a business is a micro-dictatorship with an absolute leader; in others, the boss works for the employees. Either way, you can apply consultative sales to the way you do business.

To begin, let's take a look at your current marketing strategy. How you market is a crucial component of your business philosophy, *especially* when you're stuck not selling enough. Do you market by having people come to you ("pull marketing") or by reaching out to the market and educating them about your product/service ("push marketing")? Note that with either technique, marketing is one-to-many. The single business, with its single purpose and single need, interacts with the multiple and diverse needs of the often innumerable buyers who comprise the marketplace.

Sales, on the other hand, is one-to-one. It is the salesperson's job to translate the broad appeal of marketing into the specific message for the individual buyer. Whether you use "drip (or nurture) marketing" in an effort to target specific audiences and build credibility or "wave marketing," whereby you're flooding prospects for a while (but not constantly), you'll need consultative sales to turn your marketing into transactions. This is the only approach that will shorten your sales cycle, increase your closing rate, eliminate discounting, and result in better cash flow and higher profit margins.

There are four steps in the purchase process your prospects go through:

1. The prospects recognize they have a need.

2. They decide whether to do something about it or not. (Your biggest competitor is the status quo—not taking action at all.)

3. They evaluate their options.

4. They select a vendor.

If your business sells to other businesses, however, your purchase hierarchy will be different:

1. The prospects go to their current trusted provider.

2. They ask their network.

3. They contact a recognized brand.

4. They shop around.

Either way is fine—as long as you familiarize yourself with the process of your buyers. You've got to know their process backward and forward. Once you understand that your buyers are going through a specific process, you have to match your *sales* cycle to their *buying* cycle. If you fail to recognize where they are in the process, your next step will be out of sync, with potentially disastrous results. Let me show you what I mean.

A former client ran a great catalog business in editorial training, sending out thousands of catalogs every month. After perusing the catalog, prospects called in to a salesperson who would take them through what would otherwise be a good consultative process. However, these buyers were ready to buy and didn't need a consultation. They only needed someone to answer their questions and to sign them up.

So we took the salespeople off the phone and had administration simply complete the transaction—and sales tripled. The salespeople had been getting in the way of the sale.

In short, if you're trying to recognize a buyer's process toward purchasing, you have to understand the psychology of what causes people to take action: Do people have a *compelling* reason to make a change? Does it spring from pain, fear, or pleasure? The brain is literally hardwired such that its tendency to avoid pain is 100 times greater than its tendency to seek out pleasure. That makes *pain* the easier sell. Likewise, if you're offering security, legal services, or insurance, you have to acknowledge that *fear* is what motivates your buyer.

On the other hand, you can think of *pleasure* as the buyer's vision. Plenty of people are visionaries, and want to be seen as being on the cutting edge. They have a motivation to buy as well. As a skillful salesperson, you need to discover what they want. (Remember, people buy for *their* reasons—not yours.)

Have you ever talked to a company, realized it has a problem, and wondered why the company isn't fixing it? It's often a matter of avoidance. Here's an example. You rarely treat paper cuts or minor scrapes. If you have a second-degree burn, you might apply ice or aloe vera. But if you have a broken bone, you have it set at the hospital emergency room. How many people would do a Yellow Pages analysis of healthcare facilities before they go to the emergency room? Very few, because pain compels most of them to take action. They do whatever is needed to fix the problem.

Whether it's a broken bone or a busted merger, you've got to recognize that pain, fear, or pleasure (in that order) gets people to take action, and their level of action will be proportionate to their level of pain, fear, or pleasure. Remember the videos from science class showing the amoeba moving toward the sugar and away from the vinegar? This concept is true even on a cellular level.

Selling is about relationships, so whoever builds the strongest relationship will get the deal because of trust. People buy from those whom they trust, and who are most like themselves. This dynamic actually works in your favor, because it makes it easy to tell who is a serious buyer and who is shopping around, trying to get a free education about the product and the market. If you actually have a shot at the sale, your buyers will be seeking to confide in you. But if they're only looking for information, they won't be willing to reveal anything about themselves and what they're looking for—they'll be keeping you at arm's length.

I learned this from my grandfather, who kept sheep and pigs. Sheep experience only one birth a year, and sometimes have twins. If twins are born, the mother will choose one and reject the other. My grandfather bottle-fed these rejected lambs, and he always gave them a name; one was called Lamby. When it was time to go to slaughter, he couldn't let Lamby go. In selling, when there's a relationship, your buyer is open, honest, knows your name, and you have a shot. If not, you're going to the slaughterhouse—you just don't know it yet.

Negative stereotypes about salespeople have to be resisted. When you're sick and go to the doctor, do you play a "poker game," making your doctor guess what's wrong? Of course not—you expect your doctor's questions to be personal and discovery-oriented. You then determine what you're willing to do to be cured.

That's exactly what consultative selling is: helping prospects get what they want, facilitating the cure. I think of myself as a doctor, seeking how I can help my client. But if the client is mistrustful of me as a smarmy salesperson, he will withhold the information that I need in order to help him and provide him with the best solution for his problem. Here's an example.

I was in a sales call recently where a significant amount of business was at stake. A potential client had called us hoping that we could offer her advice on going head-to-head with a large competitor that was threatening to push her out of the market. A lot was on the line for all of us: Without our help, the client was likely to go under, but if we were able to pull through for her, she'd be able to hold on to major clients that the competitor was courting, and we'd be compensated in kind.

So, I got on the line and asked, "Can you start by telling me about your business and what you know about your competitor?"

The prospect was hesitant. She gave us a taste of the situation but was clearly reluctant to divulge too much. I tried a few other questions. "How much do you know about the service your competitor is offering? What kinds of marketing have you seen it doing? What about what you're doing?"

Still, I was getting only half-answers. Slowly it began to dawn on me that the prospect was withholding crucial information because she thought she'd lose power in the relationship by letting on too much. But I had no way of offering her a solution without knowing the full scope of her problem. I said, "Listen. I understand your hesitation, but I can't help your business if I don't understand it. There's nothing at stake in your honesty but whether or not I can be of service to you."

With that simple reassurance, everything changed, and the client opened up. We found out that her situation *was* an area in which we could offer expertise, and we entered into a contract that was a win-win for both parties.

It may seem too trite a story to include in a business book. Yet I share it with you because it reinforces the image that I would like you to create for yourself: In effect, you're a physician, ministering to the needs of your patients/clients, who look to you with certainty that you are the right provider of services or goods and that they can feel safe, comfortable, and protected in your able care. But just as a doctor cannot make an accurate diagnosis without all the facts, so we businesspeople must have the courage to ask the hard questions of our clients. What's really going on? Where does it hurt? How can I help?

As a salesperson, you have to know the real story, because otherwise misunderstandings happen, and you'll make an improper diagnosis, write a premature prescription, commit malpractice. If clients are pushing you to give a recommendation without complete information, ultimately they're only preventing themselves from obtaining the best possible outcome in the transaction. They won't get the proper solution for their particular problem, and they'll be left unfulfilled.

There are three components to consultative selling: presenting, qualifying, and closing (not necessarily in that order). Let me illustrate how these components, when combined, are infinitely more powerful than any other sales approach.

Imagine there are three companies:

- Company #1 has a four-month sales cycle and a 90 percent close rate.

- Company #2 has an eight-month sales cycle and a 60 percent close rate.

- Company #3 has a fourteen-month sales cycle and a 2 percent close rate.

What does Company #1 know that the other two are missing out on?

Company #1 is employing the "Quid Pro Quo" approach to selling. It uses consultative sales by first *qualifying* the parameters of the transaction: What is the problem that needs to be solved by making this purchase? What does the client hope to accomplish with this purchase? Then, Company #1 *pre-closes* the sale, by eliciting an assurance that the client will purchase from Company #1 if it is able to deliver everything discussed in the qualifying phase. Finally, Company #1 *presents* the product/service solution.

Company #2, on the other hand, is stuck in the traditional approach, in which it qualifies, presents, then closes. It's simply not as effective.

And Company #3 presents, then qualifies, then closes—which is a very shaky tactic.

Consultative sales allows you to impress on your clients the value of the product/service *for them specifically*. If you don't do this, you have no way of differentiating what you're offering from anything else on the market. You're left with *price* as the differentiating factor, and soon you'll find yourself discounting. The drawbacks of discounting are worse than you might expect.

As you can see from this example of three hypothetical companies, the Quid Pro Quo model offers obvious benefits for you and your average client. It's ideal for large enterprises as well. Most professional buyers prefer this method because it eliminates negotiating and discounting, and it doesn't waste their time.

There are several requirements for successfully executing the Quid Pro Quo method. First, you must always remember that, at the core, it's about an effective sales process; there is no one-size-fits-all. It's not about pre-set steps, but about how successfully your salespeople sell. You also need to be able to walk away if necessary. And don't be afraid to ask tough questions. If you ask thought-provoking questions, your clients will likely need time to think about their answers before responding. Although most people are extremely uncomfortable with silence, it can actually be a very good thing.

The Quid Pro Quo approach gives you an additional opportunity to cultivate an understanding of personality types. The length of the process will differ according to the personality of your client, and thus you must learn to adapt. The questions you ask will be predicated on the type of person you're selling to. Always follow the Platinum Rule:

Treat others in the way they want to be treated.

Seek the truth of your client's needs, though you may not like what you hear. And always be prepared to say when you cannot meet a client's particular need. It's your ethical responsibility to be honest with your client about what you can and cannot do—and, moreover, to be honest with yourself.

I like to sum up the premise of consultative sales in a few easy, powerful points.

Key Points to Remember
When Doing Consultative Sales

■ You are a professional facilitator, not a salesperson.

■ Work like a doctor, winning confidence by displaying confidence in your abilities, making a thorough diagnosis of the problem, and offering your prescription without hesitation or fear of rejection.

■ Focus on the client, not on the order.

■ Not getting the deal is okay.

■ Insist on an open and honest conversation. Both you and the customer must get all your ducks in a row.

■ You and the customer must have equal business stature.

■ Play fair, or not at all.

■ Don't do bad deals.

■ They sell you—you don't sell them.

■ Believe in mutual degrees of commitment. (In other words, don't go through the process unless you know that if you lead the clients to water, they'll drink.)

Remembering these simple precepts can revolutionize your entire philosophy of sales. Soon you'll be well on your way to changing the way your sales team sells.

CHANGE THE WAY YOU ADVERTISE

Let's assume you've retrained your sales force to focus on consultative selling. Great! But that's only the beginning. When you're stuck not selling enough, more change is required of you. Much more.

After sales, the next most important factor for the majority of businesses is advertising, which is simply another method of generating prospects or sales. Most of the time, though, the advertising methods that business owners rely on are completely ineffectual—and they fail to realize this because they don't have a way of measuring the success of their ad campaigns.

Advertising has to focus on the audience, offering them a desired benefit in return for contacting you. By shifting the fundamentals of advertising and guiding your audience to immediate, direct, desirable action, you can boost sales by 30 to 50 percent or more, very quickly and with zero increase in your advertising expenditure. I like to think of effective advertising as a kind of hidden dynamite; it's a potent variable that very few businesses capitalize on. So when *you* do, you'll unleash an explosive power that can exponentially increase your sales.

If advertising is currently your main driver of sales, you can make surprisingly minor and easy changes in your existing advertising that will produce major results—and you won't have to spend a dime. There are seven leverage factors at your immediate disposal, each of which can increase sales 20 to 500 percent:

Seven Ways to Leverage Your Advertising

1. **Write Great Headlines.** No matter how good the rest of your ad is, your audience won't ever see it if they don't get past the headline. Your headline must instantly telegraph to your prospects the biggest, most appealing specific benefit or payoff they can expect to receive from contacting your company or availing themselves of your product. It must be catchy, and it must contain key words or phrases that will pop up from the page. Because your headline is so crucial, I'll go over ten examples of unbeatable headlines in a moment; but first, let's look at the remaining six tools at your disposal.

2. **Set Yourself Apart.** Distinguish your business from every other competitor by addressing an obvious void in the marketplace that you alone can honestly fill. Set your prospects' buying criteria for them, so that only you, your business, or your product can clear the bar. Focus on one specific, relevant niche that is most sorely lacking in the marketplace and make it your own.

3. **Offer Proof to Build Your Credibility.** Provide substantiation for your claims, including client testimonials, quotes from experts, and excerpts of media articles about your product. Contrast your performance, construction, or support with the competition's.

4. **Reverse Your Customers' Risk.** Put the onus on yourself. Tell your clients that you'll offer a full refund if they're not satisfied. If this isn't practical, guarantee some element of the transaction or purchase. Taking the burden of risk and uncertainty off a client will result in higher (and quicker) sales, even when you factor in the low percentage of clients who will take advantage

of the return privilege or test-drive period. I've seen companies boost their sales by more than 500 percent just by adding an incomparable, powerful, and irresistible risk reversal to the selling proposition. Most of your competition isn't addressing the marketplace's apprehension and inhibitions about buying, so you'll have the proprietary, preemptive advantage if you do.

5. **Include a Call to Action.** Now that those in your audience have read your ad or visited your website, what's next? Don't make their next step ambiguous. Your marketplace is virtually begging to be led by a trusted advisor, so take the helm and be specific. Tell them exactly what to do, why to do it, what benefits they can expect from taking action—and what dangers or penalties will result from delay. "Call now!" "Visit our store!" "Order immediately!" "Schedule a consultation!" Such phrases may sound old-school, but they're still in use for a reason.

6. **Offer a Bonus.** Whether it's a coupon, a discount, an extended warranty, an additional product or service piled on top of the basic purchase, or the promise of preferential treatment for fast-actors ("Be one of the first five callers and receive a free companion book!" "Be a charter VIP/Platinum member with priority attention guaranteed for life!"), a bonus on top of your already fabulous product or service proposition can only further entice and multiply sales.

7. **Summarize Your Offer.** By summarizing your offer at the end of your ad, you are seizing the moment to "bring it home": Reiterate the problem you are able to solve, the benefits your buyers will gain, and the upside with no downside. Then tell them again how to act now.

CHANGE YOUR ADVERTISING HEADLINES

If you've ever been to a rock concert, you know that the opening act is just a warm-up for the main event. But you're there for one reason only: to see the headliner.

The headlines of your advertising are equally important. The right headline will make the crowd go wild.

When you sit down to write your headline, or when you review the headline submitted to you by your copywriter, it will help to have in mind some highly successful examples that have yielded results for other businesses. Here are ten of my favorites, drawn with permission from Victor O. Schwab's vital book, *How to Write a Good Advertisement.**

Ten Terrific Advertising Headlines
That Delivered Great Business Results

1. **"How to Win Friends and Influence People."** This headline helped to sell millions of copies of the now-famous book by the same title. It has strong, obvious appeal: We all want to win friends and influence people. But without the words "How to," the headline would have become simply a trite wall motto.

2. **"A Little Mistake That Cost a Farmer $3,000 a Year."** A sizable appropriation was successfully spent on placing this ad in farm magazines. Sometimes the negative idea of offsetting, reducing, or eliminating the "risk of loss" is even more attractive to the reader than the "prospect of gain." As railroad executive (back

---

*Originally published by Wilshire Books in 1985, the paperback edition is available on Amazon.com and I recommend that you run, not walk, to the nearest computer and order a copy posthaste.

when that meant something!) and U.S Senator Chauncey Depew once said, "I would not stay up all of one night to make $100; but I would stay up all of seven nights to keep from losing it."

And as Walter Norvath notes in *Six Successful Selling Techniques*, "People will fight much harder to avoid losing something they already own than to gain something of greater value that they do not own." It's also true that most people feel it's easier to retrieve losses and waste than to gain new profits. Capitalize on this.

3. **"Are You Ever Tongue-Tied at a Party?"** This headline pinpoints the myriad self-conscious wallflowers out there, people who will read it and say, "This is talking to me!" You'll also notice that it's interrogative. It asks a question—and people will want to read the answer. It excites curiosity and interest in the body matter that follows, and it hits home, cutting through verbose indirectness.

   The best interrogative headlines are challenges that are difficult to ignore, cannot be dismissed with a quick no or yes, and—even without further reading—are immediately pertinent and relevant to the reader.

4. **"Do You Make These Mistakes in English?"** Again, a direct challenge. Now read the headline again, eliminating the vital word "These." This word is the hook that almost forces you into the copy. "What are these particular mistakes?" the prospect thinks. "Do I make them?" Also notice that this headline promises to provide helpful personal information in its own context, not merely as "advertising talk." This is what I call the "attraction of the specific." You see how magnetically it helps to draw the reader into the body matter of an advertisement.

   Many of the best headlines contain specific words or phrases that make a promise to tell you one or all of the following: *how, here's, these, which, which of these, who, who else, where, when, what, why.* Also enormously catching is the use of specific amounts: *the number of days, evenings, hours, minutes, dollars, ways, types of.*

This "attraction of the specific" is worth your special attention, not only with respect to words and phrases but also concerning headline ideas themselves. For example, compare the appeal of *"We'll Help You Make More Money"* with *"We'll Help You Pay the Rent."*

5. **"When Doctors 'Feel Rotten,' This Is What They Do."** What's the secret of the success of this well-known ad? First, there's the suggestion of paradox, because we seldom think of doctors as being in poor health themselves. And when they are, what they do about it is information right from the horse's mouth; it carries a note of authority and greater assurance of a reward for reading the ad. Note the positive promise of reward in *"This Is What They Do."*

Second, the use of the unabashed colloquialism *"Feel Rotten"* gets attention; it sounds human, natural. It also has surprise value, because advertising pages ordinarily have a certain stilted quality. Many headlines fail to stop readers because their vocabulary is so hackneyed; their words, expressions, and ideas are merely those in common use. Indeed, this ad pulled only half the number of responses when a test was made that changed *"When Doctors 'Feel Rotten'"* to *"When Doctors Don't Feel Up to Par."*

Since the idea of using "unexpected" headline words is worth such serious consideration, let's look at a few more examples.

■ For a book on scientific weight control: the word "pot-belly." Not very elegant, but it proved an effective stopper.

- For a dictionary: a single word ("onion," "hog," "shad," "pelican," "skunk," "kangaroo," etc.) as the boldface headline of each in a series of small-space advertisements. You couldn't miss it on the page, and you wanted to know what it was all about. The copy followed through by illustrating how simple and clear the definitions in that particular dictionary were.

- For a book on golf instruction: "Don't Bellyache About Your Golf This Year!"

6. **"Guaranteed to Go Through Ice, Mud, or Snow—Or We Pay the Tow!"** If you offer a powerful guarantee with your product, play it up strongly and quickly in the headline. Don't relegate it to minor display. Many products are actually backed up by dramatic guarantees—but their advertising does not make the most of them. And, of course, it doesn't hurt that this ad rhymes.

7. **"Is the Life of a Child Worth $1 to You?"** This trenchant headline was used by a brake-relining service. It has strong emotional appeal, prompting people to think about how the life of a little child could be snuffed out by an accident caused by *their* ineffective brakes.

8. **"Six Types of Investors—Which Group Are You In?"** This ad produced inquiries in large quantities. Investors reviewed the characteristics of each of the six groups described in the ad, then inquired about a program designed to meet the investment purposes of their own group.

    This headline also illustrates "the primary viewpoint," or the "point of you." Many highly engaging headlines contain one of the following words—"you," "your," or "yourself." Even when the pronoun is first-person singular (for example, *"How I*

Improved My Memory in One Evening"), the reward promised is so universally desired that, in effect, it is saying, "You can do it, too!"

Here's a statistic that proves the power of the "point of you": In a study during which 500 women were given a fountain pen, 96 percent wrote their own names; and when shown a map of the United States, 447 men out of 500 looked first for the location of their home towns! Howard Barnes, of the American Newspaper Publishers' Association, really got it right when he said: "To call up an image of the reader, all you need to do is pin up a target. Then, starting at the outside, you can label his interests in this order: the world, the United States, his home state, his home town, and we'll lump together in the black center his family and himself . . . *me*. Myself. I come first. I am the bull's eye."

9. **"For the Woman Who Is Older Than She Looks."** This headline was a stopper for thousands of women—and proved more successful than the subtly different *"For the Woman Who Looks Younger Than She Is."*

10. **"Announcing . . . The New Edition of the Encyclopedia That Makes It Fun to Learn Things."** The announcement type of headline (when bringing out a new product) wins attention because people are interested in new things. Look for phrases like "new kind of," "new discovery," "new way to," and so on. Americans love the new or novel; for them, the mere factor of newness seems to be prima facie evidence of "betterness."

Undeviating affection for the old and proven may be strong in other countries; in ours, the desire to try the new is stronger. The great achievements of our inventors and enterprising manufacturers have trained us to believe that if it's new, it's likely to be better. However, the word "new" in a headline should be backed up by copy pointing out the merits of something really new and advantageous, not merely different.

Headlines pack a lot of power in their punch. Just a few well-chosen words can launch your business far beyond the doldrums of not selling enough into a world where calls from clients just won't stop. The right headline can only underline your business's success.

CHANGE YOUR ONLINE PRESENCE

In this day and age, it's imperative that you have an online presence. If you don't already have a website, you might as well open a stall at Indy's Egyptian bazaar.

In 2006, a little-known U.S. senator launched a campaign for the presidency. As a fundamental part of his campaign, the senator utilized the Internet to a degree greater than that of any other candidate in the general election for president of the United States. The official campaign website offered an array of special features, including the option to make financial contributions online. His campaign also utilized viral marketing and networking, sending out frequent mass e-mails and even posting videos on YouTube.

The result? Senator Barack Obama became the forty-fourth president of the United States.

The power of the World Wide Web should not be underestimated. Almost every company with an online presence is generating revenue from it, or at least some strategic, profitable advantage. If you don't have an online presence, get one. Although I can't make any promises regarding a presidential bid, I can guarantee that your business is better off online than offline.

Here are some general guidelines you can use as a launching pad for your site—but keep in mind that building a website is a tall order and goes far beyond the scope of this book. The next few paragraphs will give you a handle on the most important aspects to be aware of, as well as the areas where you could run into common pitfalls.

If you already have a website or some other form of web presence (like a marketplace on eBay), the first step you have to take is to do the research to find out how your clients are finding you. Are they coming across your site via search engines? Or are you getting hits from paid searches? If clients are finding you through keywords or paid advertising, make certain that your current ads and propositions consist of benefit-based headlines or phrases that telegraph the biggest, most desirable, and specific payoff(s) the client can get from visiting your website.

Next, take a hard look at your actual website—as if you were the prospect or visitor. Be sure that your homepage introduces your business benefit up front. Web users visit websites out of *self-interest*, so you need to make certain that your homepage's headline communicates the biggest payoff they'll get from staying there and going deeper. Beyond that, the payoff you communicate has to be better and more desirable than what they can get from visiting other, similar sites—or from finding another means of addressing their business problem.

You want to design your website in a very simple but lucid manner. The moment visitors arrive, they must make an immediate connection to your product or service, or to your company in general. They need to be captivated, drawn in, and motivated to stay there. They need to see right from the start the wonderful benefit of what you're selling and what it will do for them or their business: how it will address their needs, wants, problems, challenges, and frustrations, and give them a better tomorrow.

The next step is to lead them through an obvious progression of the information they'll be viewing—an overview, client testimonials, and other added value such as risk reversal or bonuses—before they take the ultimate step in making a purchase. Because certain visitors will need more or less information than others, your design needs to be *pragmatic, sequential, progressive,* and *logical.* At any point along this progression, the website visitor should be able to skip the rest of the information and proceed directly to the purchase, or select the option to request more information, or schedule a call/consultation appointment. This means you should have, on every page of your site, a direct-to-purchase link.

Remember: We live in the era of convenience. *The easier you make it for your clients, the more likely they are to buy.*

CHANGE HOW YOU LEVERAGE

In Chapter 2, we talked about how to beat out the competition. But other businesses and businesspeople aren't always the opposition. If you have the right perspective, you'll see how they can actually help you sell more. Employing the collaborative help of others is crucial to your success. In fact, it's so crucial that I devote an entire chapter to it later in the book (Chapter 10: Are You Stuck Still Saying "I Can Do It Myself"?). But for the time being, let's take a brief look at what it means to leverage the resources of other people—and how this can help you increase sales specifically.

Some businesspeople want to do it all themselves. I can tell you that this will rarely, if ever, achieve the optimal result. It might have been the old ideal, and you might have gotten used to thinking of it as noble, but it's ineffective. It costs you productivity, profitability, and positioning. Leveraging, on the other hand, *is* effective.

People often don't know how to masterfully leverage themselves through other people. Keep in mind that it is rare for one business to be completely self-sufficient. Never have I seen a business that possesses, on its own, *all* the skills needed for optimal functioning. It just doesn't happen.

Executive coach Robert Hargrove once said that the defining trait of the greatest entrepreneur in the twenty-first century will be his or her ability to creatively collaborate with other people. You will never acquire all of the necessary skills yourself. So long as there are only twenty-four hours in a day, it simply isn't possible—not in our new, fast-paced world with its rapidly evolving knowledge base. (Our body of knowledge supposedly doubles every six months.)

Here are what I think of as the ABCs of the myriad resources other people can provide you with: advertisements, advice, agencies, assets, associates, associations, back-end products, beliefs, bonuses, buying power, cash, collateral, connections, credibility, data, databases, enthusiasm, equity, goodwill, hard assets, human resources, ideas, imagination, influence, intangible assets, investments, knowledge, leads, lists, management, markets, mastermind groups, money, opportunities, patents, people, products, promotions, R&D, relationships, relative strengths, sales force, skills, systems, testimonials, values, wholesalers—and the list goes on. It's limited only by your vision. Tap into the leverage that can be found in creative collaboration by finding others who offer pieces of the knowledge, skill, influence, access, or relationship puzzle that you are missing.

The best way to achieve extraordinary greatness, then, is to leverage yourself and your assets off the assets and access of others. If you can give them what they want, they will, in turn, richly reward you with whatever it is you want, as long as you're clear on precisely what this is.

Leveraging requires that you be the first and, optimally, only person who enables the people you leverage through seeing what they truly want but haven't gotten, why they want it, and how they can get it—with your help. Sometimes it's acknowledgment. At other times it's intellectual stimulation. For some, it's purely the idea of mining themselves. For others, it's compensation tied to how their contribution performs.

It is truly possible to build an empire by leveraging yourself through others. I have seen it done many times. Here's just one example.

My friend Marc Goldman once shared with me a fantastic, inventive tale of joint venturing. He had a podiatrist who didn't realize his practice was leveraging a joint venture. The podiatrist had been renting office space, and when his lease expired, he had bills to pay just like the rest of us, and he couldn't afford to move to the nicer space that he wanted.

But he happened to find a sleep clinic in a fantastic part of town that was open only from 6:00 in the evening until 6:00 in the morning, and he negotiated the use of the property when the clinicians weren't there. From 7:00 in the morning until about 5:00 in the evening, he had the space. He worked out a deal whereby he agreed to pay half the rent and half the utilities, and he got the place for less than half of what he was originally going to pay for a renewal of his old lease.

Do you need a sales force? Find somebody who's got a sales force that isn't being fully utilized in your field and isn't directly competitive, and do a joint venture with this person and share profits. Need a warehouse? Find somebody who's got excess storage space or delivery capability and do a joint venture for a share of the growth you'll both experience. You can only stand to gain when you engineer performance- and result-based partnering deals like these.

Each of us is limited—by time, by ability, by resources, by access. However, when you leverage yourself through others, you're limited only by your vision and ability to harness the incredible force you've created. You can do anything. If you're willing to structure inventive new relationships and associations, you can leverage yourself to access enormous market potential by finding other businesses or individuals who already enjoy direct, trusted access to the resources you need. You can leverage for technological growth. You can leverage for capital or its equivalent. Figure out what you'd do with the capital if you had it, and then joint-venture with somebody who's already got it and has an excess capacity, or somebody who's already got the big product for which you need capital to purchase.

You can even leverage to overcome your fear of spending money. The good news is you don't have to spend a dime. You can leverage off other people's expenditures. There is always, in any situation, somebody else who's got a problem that you're the solution for.

A common misperception is that you have to spend lots of cash to inject new life into your existing business. Let me be the first to tell you: It simply isn't true. What you have to do is learn how to harness and access other people's efforts and assets. What is it you want? Whatever you want, somebody else has it in excess capacity, right now. Look at commonalities. Here's an example.

Years ago when I was in the collectibles business, the first thing we did was find people who collected coins so we could find out what else they collected. As it turned out, about 70 percent of them also collected guns and wildlife art. We were able to approach companies in those markets with joint ventures to access not just hundreds but *250,000* new clients from that one inquiry. And the best part: We paid these sources only out of the results. We never paid for speculative advertising.

A client from China who attended one of our seminars wanted to go international but, in order to do so, needed to improve his skill set, management prowess, and capital. He was a reasonably successful businessman in motorcycle manufacturing, so he went to Indonesia and Malaysia and found people in similar areas of manufacturing who had successful distribution networks and manufacturing capability. He joint-ventured with them and built a

$10 million motorcycle business in one year—with no manufacturing, no employees, nothing more than the assets he already possessed.

Could this businessman have accomplished the same goal on his own? Not likely. Even if this were possible, it certainly would have taken him a lot longer. Indiana Jones may have been able to save himself from certain dismemberment with nothing but his trusty pistol, but in the real world, things work a little differently. If you can harness the power of leveraging and use it to its maximum potential, you'll learn how to beat the seven-foot giants without so much as breaking a sweat.

CHANGE YOUR MESSAGE: MAKE WHATEVER YOU OFFER IRRESISTIBLE TO PROSPECTIVE CLIENTS

So you've changed your sales methodology to consultative sales, you've revitalized your advertising, you've got a killer new headline, and your website is getting several hundred hits a day. And yet, when you checked your metrics from the last quarter, you were stunned to see that you're still stuck not selling enough. What's the deal?

Let's first consider your Internet presence. To increase your online sales, you have to convert more of your current-site *visitors* into *buyers*. I can tell you from experience that the reason most businesses don't enjoy this outcome is that their message isn't compelling. Their value isn't unique and distinctive, and so their offer is resistible. You want your offer to be *irresistible*.

Your business's message is the overarching umbrella under which all the other components—your advertising, your sales approach, your headlines—reside. It's the intangible quality that lingers with your potential clients after they meet you, or after they walk away from your booth at a trade show, or after your well-crafted advertisement first catches their eye in the local paper. Your message is also what makes leveraging possible:

It's what attracts potential partners and collaborators to your cause.

As noted above, your offer needs to be irresistible. Your message has to spring directly from what you want to accomplish. What do you want to deliver to your market? And what are you really capable of delivering? Determine the answers to these questions and, from there, make your offer captivating, poignant, *and* logical—because the vast majority of prospects you reach will be logical themselves.

Logical people will throw what I call the "So what?" curveball into your game. They will listen, watch, read, and then experience your sales proposition and dynamic. Your website has to break things down clearly, concisely, and directly, or those people are going to say "So what?" and leave.

You need to make sure your message leaves no room for that phrase even to cross any potential client's mind. Show your prospects that you appreciate, understand, respect, and empathize with their situation, problems, or desires; that's how you create a strong, lasting rapport. Every element of your message must resonate with their mindset, so that they feel you understand them better than any of your competitors do.

If you're planning to host a booth at a trade show, identify the people you want to reach and send them a pre-invitation. As always, focus on the payoff of visiting you: You've got to promise them something really valuable that will stick in their mind (whether it's a benefit, a bit of exclusive information, or a superior product) so they won't forget to visit your booth.

Most people blow opportunities at trade shows by having ineffective signs. The sign is like your headline. Change it, and you can exponentially increase the quantity and quality of traffic at your booth. Your prospects need to be able to easily and quickly see who you are, what services or products you provide, what benefits you have to offer—and why they should choose you above the competition.

For example, if your banner says "Production Management Tools That Increase Profitability by 30 Percent or More, Guaranteed," you will certainly draw desirable attention. No one can say "So what?" to that. It is important to capitalize on every situation and every process that you identify. But by telegraphing the right promise to exactly the right prospect, you are promoting a logical mentality—one that mirrors your buyer's. Try walking in his or her shoes (and I'll tell more about how to do this in Chapter 8).

Signage is the headline for the benefits you're offering; it's the ultimate reason people will visit your booth. Then, when your prospects actually arrive, you have thirty seconds to nail your point home. When the stakes are high and the moment is *now*, you've got to be able to convey to your potential client why she should give you another five or ten minutes, especially when there are 2,000 other booths all vying for her time and attention. You've got to understand the game you're playing— the brutal, competitive, clawing game of selling products and services. You can always win—and even dominate—in this little-understood arena if you take such advice to heart.

Your game requires a higher level of brinksmanship and strategic mastery than the old-school notion of the product pusher—the door-to-door, "schmoozing" salesperson with a canned spiel. It's about adding more real value and demonstrating clear understanding of what's important to your buyer. It's also about respecting and empathically grasping the mind of your client and the needs of the market, so that you're the only really viable provider. You have to understand the problems that people are having, create a brilliant solution, and express both in well-defined, dimensional ways. That's the message you need to send.

It all boils down to the strategy of preeminence, which I introduced in Chapter 2 and will discuss further in Chapter 8. The idea of having a unique selling proposition (i.e., something you project to your prospects that favorably differentiates you from all the other direct and indirect competition) gives way to a more elevated and preemptive concept: being the only viable solution *and* the most trusted advisor to the market or market segment you serve. Today, finding a unique niche requires more than being seen as the only viable solution. Having a unique selling proposition can be very powerful, but being unique isn't enough. You also have to be trustworthy.

You can achieve this by first setting your market's buying criteria and, second, by demonstrating that your product, service, or business can better fulfill your market's goal or desire than that of anyone else your prospects could turn to. Find out what your market *really* wants and needs, then show them why you are the only practical, logical, viable option for fulfillment.

Consider your own wants and needs. Of course you want to be different, but, more important, you want to be needed as a person and as a business. To bring this about, you have to clearly articulate what is otherwise ambiguous and unclear to the buyer—that you are the *only* path to fulfillment for your market. Make that your message, and the sales will start piling in.

CHANGE IS THE NAME OF THE GAME

Did you know that, in a bad market, you can take 15 to 20 percent of the business away from many of your top competitors, obtain 20 to 30 percent of all the new business coming in, and achieve 30 to 40 percent more sales conversions from the people who are coming to you? I'm not pulling these numbers out of thin air; I've seen them in action time and again. You do the math—the growth is geometrical. That's change you can believe in.

Stuck not selling enough? Time to dust off your pistol and change the game. Because as Bruce Barton, the advertising legend who created Betty Crocker, said: "When you are through changing, you are through."

Let's hope you're never "through." But when it comes to dealing with the changing nature of an erratic business volume—*that's* the time to put up a fight. And in the next chapter, I'll show you how.

The Bottom Line

■ Change the way your salespeople sell by training them in consultative selling.

■ People buy because they place their trust in their relationship with you. Consultative sales cultivates that trust.

■ The basis of consultative sales is the Quid Pro Quo approach. First *qualify* the parameters of the transaction, then *pre-close* the sale by ensuring that your customer will buy if you can deliver, and finally *present* your product or service.

■ Shift your advertising so that it focuses on the audience.

■ In your ads: Write great headlines, set yourself apart, build your credibility, reverse your customer's risk, include a call to action, offer a bonus, and then summarize your offer.

■ If you don't have an online presence, *get one*. If you do, *optimize it*.

■ Your website must be pragmatic: Make it easy for your clients to buy.

■ Sell more through inventive relationships and associations. If you're lacking resources, joint-venture with those who aren't.

- ■ Make your offer irresistible by leaving no room for your customer to say "So what?"

- ■ As always, change your approach—that's the only way to change your results.

☞ **Immediate Action Step** Stop being afraid of your clients and prospects. Recognize the power inherent in asking them questions. Your M.D. isn't afraid to ask you questions about your health—and, for that matter, would be unable to diagnose you properly without the full picture. So shift your mindset from supplicant to physician and ask—respectfully and thoughtfully—every question you need to ask in order to understand your client's situation. Your client will respect you for it!

4

ARE YOU STUCK WITH ERRATIC BUSINESS VOLUME?

Years ago, Colonial Penn Life Insurance started as an insurance company focused on selling group programs through affinity markets. Back in the 1950s, the executives at Colonial Penn sat in the boardroom racking their brains over how to attract new affinity groups. (And before your eyes glaze over with a story that seems six decades old, bear with me: Discovering how Colonial Penn solved this problem is worth waiting for.) The company's execs were seeking alumni associations and other large organizations with a common purpose, but they just weren't having any luck. The field was very competitive, and they were having a lot of trouble persuading organizations to buy their insurance. Some people expressed an interest; others didn't. In the flux of the market, the company was edging precariously along, never sure if it was going to make a sale.

So what did the Colonial Penn execs do? They came up with a brilliant idea. They said, "Okay, let's start our own organization, so we can become our own captive clients." The time commitment and cost expenditures were relatively small, and this new organization would allow the company to better target the senior population.

To many people at the time, it seemed like a crazy idea. But that crazy idea would make Colonial Penn one of the most profitable companies in the United States, according to *Forbes* magazine. Fast-forward a few years: Today they're doing billions in business, and other organizations are now seeking *them* out to create plans.

What the Colonial Penn execs did was establish a method for counteracting the erratic business volume they were experiencing. They essentially devised a plan of counterattack. They shifted their strategy away from the old paradigm of trying to win business away from other companies that already had programs in place. Before, they were stuck frantically playing defense against a fluctuating marketplace. Now, they had switched to playing offense, creating their own captive, loyal, long-term mega-client that generated billions of dollars of premium income for Colonial Penn—with no competition.

In this chapter, I'll teach you how to unstick yourself from a cycle of erratic business volume. It's all about developing a successful migration strategy for advancing and enhancing relationships with buyers, as well as referrers and endorsers. That's exactly what the Colonial Penn executives did when they created their own organization.

That organization, by the way, was the American Association of Retired People (AARP). Ever heard of it?

STRATEGIZE, ANALYZE, AND SYSTEMIZE YOUR BUSINESS

In the last chapter, we talked about how to change your tactics when you're not selling enough. But what if sometimes you *are* selling enough, and sometimes you aren't? What if there seems to be no way to predict how much business you bring in on a regular basis?

A lot of businesses are asking these questions, especially as the economy itself is in a state of flux. A number of companies find themselves at the mercy of an unpredictable volume of sales. But that doesn't mean *you* have to be.

The biggest problem for small- to medium-sized businesses can be summed up in three sentences:

1. They're not *strategic*.

2. They're not *analytical*.

3. They're not *systematic*.

Businesses should take only those actions that always—not sometimes, but *always*—advance and enhance the long-term, well-reasoned game plan of attracting prospects, converting them to clients, and creating a lasting, repeat-buying relationship with them. Anything that impedes this logical progression is a chink in your business's armor.

Let's say you're a farmer who grows a single crop. You wouldn't grow corn this year and decide on a different crop the following year—not as long as corn is still a viable, profitable, economically desirable commodity. And you certainly wouldn't assume that, the following year, you could stop watering and fertilizing your corn and just let it grow on its own since—heck—it did fine the previous year.

The same is true with your client base. The mere fact that your client has made one purchase doesn't mean he should now be left alone, on the assumption that he'll make a second purchase and all future re-purchases on his own, with no help, guidance, direction, or instruction from you or your sales force. Now that you have a strong, valuable asset in this client, you must strategically and systematically nurture the relationship.

Allow it to grow and flourish under your direction so that it can aid in sustaining and enriching your business.

Strategizing, analyzing, and systemizing: These are the three keys to busting the erratic business volume blues. It's that simple—as easy as one, two, three.

Now let's break them down even further.

KNOW YOUR BUSINESS *STRATEGY* FOR BRINGING IN PROSPECTS OR CLIENTS

If you're not strategic, then each month you'll be putting out the same fires. Usually those fires are related to finances and cash flow. If you're like most businesses without a workable strategy, you'll find yourself rehashing the same problem time after time: how to get through that month and pay the rent. Every thirty days, you start over, interminably pushing that same boulder up the same slippery hillside.

However, if you're strategic, every month sees your business bringing in clients and prospects at a predictable rate from the best performing sources you've identified as the most viable. You have an unshakable system in place that progressively and sequentially moves your prospects down an evolutionary line: A lead or prospect gets converted to a first-time buyer (ideally a multi-product or -service buyer in the first transaction), then he becomes a repeat buyer, then he evolves into a more advanced buyer, and so on. And along the way, he stimulates referrals, who then get moved along the same evolutionary line. Each new referral grows in his or her purchasing capacity *and* helps you attract new clients. Before you know it, your business is expanding prosperously in all directions at once.

We'll take a closer look at strategizing in Chapter 5, but for now let's go over a few key points. When it comes to how to create your initial strategy, we'll start at the very beginning. The first question you have to ask yourself is this:

*What kind of people or businesses do you want
your business to attract, and why?*

Your strategy will change according to your target audience; clearly, you'll need to strategize differently to reach different kinds of clients. For example, online models tend to attract new prospects in droves, but these new prospects are usually generic, indefinable masses—promiscuous buyers, perhaps, but indiscriminate and disloyal ones as well. Are you better off attracting waves of unknowns? Or will it behoove you to have fewer but far better-defined and more motivated prospects, people who are eager to embark on a relationship based on the strategically formulated buying criteria you've clearly established? If you can't or don't paint a clear portrait for yourself of whom you're trying to attract and why, you're not going to get them as buyers.

So how do you go about defining and understanding your marketplace? The short answer is that you'll have to do some basic marketplace research—the springboard for any effective business strategy. It doesn't have to be a complex process, nor does it need to be costly. It can be as simple and as easy as surveying a cross-section of your consumers (a focus group) to get their opinions about the product or service you offer, or conducting a telephone or mail survey. The disadvantage of using the telephone or mail survey method is, of course, that the individuals you contact may not be interested in responding to a survey. Therefore, I suggest getting creative: Offer a coupon or bonus in exchange for a completed survey, or save the survey for the end of a successful sales call, when your satisfied client might be more than happy to offer her thoughts in return for a positive sales experience.

As you lay the groundwork for your strategy, your primary focus should be on gathering enough information to find out the following:

- Who are your best potential clients?

- What do they need, want, and expect?

- Is there a demand for your product or service?

- Who are your competitors, and how well are they doing?

You should strive to answer these basic questions specifically and in detail.

For example, if you're in real estate, you want to know how many houses are sold each year in your market and how much money is spent in your area. Or, if you're selling luxury watches, investigate the comparable watches on the market, and look at the numbers to see how well they're selling. Examine the demographics of your target audience so that you know what they need; then position yourself as the best person to fulfill that need.

For any industry, you want to find out how many units are sold or how much is spent; this helps you gauge your performance success against the competition and enables you to set specific goals. You also want to know how these numbers have changed over the last few decades. Have there been any major trends? Most trade journals that cover a particular industry do an "annual wrap-up" on the industry, which can be invaluable.

Although market research may appear to be a tedious, time-consuming process, it is necessary if you want to be successful. Think of it as simply a method of finding out what catches clients' attention—specifically, by observing their actions and drawing conclusions from what you see. It's an organized way of finding objective answers to questions every business owner and manager must answer in order to succeed.

After you've identified the people in your target market, it's time to take the next step in your strategy: Define exactly

what problem your product or service solves for those particular people. This is where you turn inward to look for commonalities in your existing client base that represent the most
desirable and profitable buyers you have. Your goal is to
replicate, multiply, and perpetuate a constant flow of this
market segment—above and beyond all other categories you
could attract. I've boiled this down to a simple example,
which admittedly might be a bit more obvious than what
you're likely to run into in your industry, but it'll help you see
the idea clearly.

Suppose you sell bicycles, and you've analyzed your active and inactive client
base for your business and found that, lo and behold, among your 3,000
clients from every demographic and marketing source, 350 have the word
"Doctor" in front of their names on the data listing. Not something you were
expecting: None of your marketing materials were aimed at doctors, yet
somehow that's who your business has heavily attracted.

So, in your next round of targeted marketing, you now target doctors,
knowing that they have a higher motivation and predisposition toward buying
bicycles and buying them from your business, and therefore should be easier
to convert. You've figured out both what you're offering and to whom your offering has maximum appeal.

Strategic businesses have ongoing systems that are constantly converting clients. They have carefully analyzed their
sales data to find quantitative data connecting the correlations
between different types of prospects or buyers and different
origins. They know where the big vein of profit exists, and they
dig there first and foremost. Analyzing data allows a business
to say, for example, that if a prospect comes in through an ad
in the *Los Angeles Times* and buys a $50 widget, the statistical
probability is that she will buy four or more $100 items within
the next year, and four more the following year.

The sad truth is that few businesses actually do this. Whether
it's because they're not aware that they should, don't know the

process to use, or are simply lazy, most business owners never put into place a highly targeted, prime-prospect lead generation and conversion strategy based on analyzing the empirical (i.e., historical) data they've already experienced that allows them to project their growth. Here's another story, from the era when Krugerrands were still legal for Americans to purchase.

I used to work in the gold bullion business, where we sold gold bars, platinum, and silver ingots and coins. We knew with a high degree of certainty that one out of every four leads emanating from certain financial newsletters would convert in approximately sixty days—*if* we did a sequence of strategically formulated follow-up activities: generally a call, followed by a letter, followed by a call.

We also knew that the first sale would, at worst, still result in a certain predictable, minimum amount of profit, and that out of every ten of those first-time buyers, six would buy again within a few months at a much higher level, thus producing a much richer subsequent profit for our business. The projections were conservative, but they allowed us to take certain steps that we otherwise would not have felt comfortable taking, such as hiring more employees, investing in the redesign of the educational newsletters that brought clients in, or generating more newsletter-originated prospects to put through our conversion pipeline system.

The other thing we knew was that if we had very, very good months, we could go deeper into future profit expectation (thus allowing us to spend more, now knowing it would come back later). We had other, slower-gestating but longer-yielding promotions that we could call on when we had months of extraordinarily good cash flow, and we could set even more future profit flow in motion for the future.

In short, we knew an awful lot. And that kind of knowledge allowed us to streamline our strategy to eliminate the elements of uncertainty with which so many businesses contend.

An effective business strategy never goes stale. Instead, it continues to progress and evolve alongside your business. Part of strategizing is projecting ahead and planning for the next phase of success. That way, your ship continues to sail smoothly, regardless of the gales and tempests plaguing your competitor's fleet. Let's go back to our bicycle example.

Suppose you've already sold 10,000 bikes this year, 5,000 of them to doctors. But don't stop there. Would the next logical progression be to sell these doctors another hobby or recreation, or perhaps something in the realm of health, fitness, or nutrition? This first question paves the way for a second one: *What other products or services does that category of influence logically buy?* If your clients are primarily in the medical profession, they most likely buy upscale items, such as art, prestige travel packages, sports cars, or custom-designed furniture.

By asking yourself these two questions, you can identify which other companies have (and sell) those kinds of products or services. Are you better off passing the business on to them in the form of an endorsement or referral, perhaps in exchange for a generous percentage of revenue and reciprocal referrals? Or is it better to keep the relationship you've worked so hard to maintain and to make the direct offer yourself?

Neither answer is right or wrong. It depends entirely on the specific factors of your business situation and the technical elements of any product/service offering you're thinking of adding. Your biggest challenge is to make a decision. But isn't that a great challenge to have for the opportunity of maybe doubling, even re-doubling your profit potential every year? Now that's the beauty of a winning strategy!

KNOW HOW TO *ANALYZE* WAYS OF GETTING BUSINESS

After strategizing, the second thing you have to do to combat erratic business volume is to analyze the life of your business. Most business owners don't have a clue about the long-term meaning of "business life." They don't analyze the value of leads or sales that come from the various sources they are using, such as ads, sales letters, or search engines. But this kind of analysis is critical to getting your business unstuck. You're never going to move forward and upward unless you take the time to analyze what has or hasn't moved the dial in the past. Let's look at a real-world example.

I once had a client group consisting of clinicians whose business was bioidentical hormones, the supplemental use of synthetic hormones for such purposes as wellness and perceived youthfulness. They frequently ran ads in the *Los Angeles Times*, then pulled the ads once they stopped seeing an up-front profit. When I was called in to review the business and analyze their numbers and metrics, I asked their reason for stopping when they broke even. The excuse I received was "If we spend $6,000 on the ad, and we get only $6,000 in new clients, we've lost money."

So I crunched the numbers, made real projections based on past patient-treatment history, and asked them what their strategy was based on. When they said they just wanted patients, I told them that was an inefficient strategy, that they should instead have a strategy based on their different kinds of treatment programs. It turns out they never looked at their advertising that way.

They had three fundamental treatment programs, one requiring visits every month; another, every quarter; and a third, every six months. These three treatments were worth, per client, $10,000, $5,000, and $3,000 a year, respectively. First-time consultations were $300. When the clinicians ran a $6,000 ad, they considered it breaking even to bring in twenty new, first-time clients/patients.

However, after analyzing their data, I came back with a different view. If we broke down the twenty new consultations into the three areas of treatment, roughly six would be worth $10,000 a year, for at least one year and possibly two. That adds up to $60,000 in Year 1 alone—and that's 100 percent profit on just one-third of the new patients alone, because the clinic has already broken even on the ad with the initial consultation. Another six new patients will come in for Treatment 2 for $5,000 a year, which means an additional $30,000, bringing us up to $90,000. The final six new patients will be worth—at least—$3,000 each, for a total of $18,000. Let's say half of them will return for a second year, bringing the total profit for Treatment 3 up to $45,000.

In total, what the clinicians thought was just a "break-even ad" was actually bringing in roughly $135,000 of pure profit annually.

They now viewed their little *L.A. Times* ad in a whole new light. I showed them that they could run it as long as the ad was attracting the right quality and category of treatment-based patient. It would continue to keep the money flowing in for years to come. And that's just one ad!

This sort of "quantification analysis" applies not only to ads but also to where you sell, what you sell, and the subsequent products offered (and purchased) after you convert a client. Unless you analyze what you don't realize that you already know, you won't know where to make the best investment—not to spend money but to *invest* it. In short, everything you're doing should be a strategic investment in the future, made with the optimal long-term, financial, and strategic business returns in mind.

So, how can you know where your salespeople should concentrate their time? If you're looking at just the present moment, you're going to see only how much money they can put in the bank for you today. That's a case of leaving a whole pile of future profits on the table—or what I like to call a "positive iceberg."

If I instead said "negative iceberg," you might already have some sense of what I mean. Picture in your mind the shipmate on the *Titanic* who spotted the peak of the iceberg too late. A positive iceberg is just as easy to imagine, when you take the time to think about its potency. It's when you see a pointed, immediate problem but don't realize that, by nurturing or harnessing it in a more long-term, strategic way, you can develop it into massive regenerative profits that can continually flow from the original source. In my example above, $6,000 was just the tip of the iceberg in terms of what the clinic was pulling in as profit from one ad—and my client group might have stopped running that ad altogether had they not been shown the mammoth iceberg lying just below the surface. When I calculated their return on investment, or ROI (which we'll discuss in more depth in Chapter 6), that ad was delivering 2,000 percent annual return on their modest $6,000 investment.

Businesses can't avail themselves of this type of information if they don't clearly and carefully analyze their data. It's not hard. Yet, almost no small- to medium-sized business does this. Here's another example.

I had a smaller client with an arcade below the boardwalk in a local California tourist hangout comprising several dozen funky little retail shops. Some quick data analysis revealed that each person who visited the arcade spent roughly $5. This means that a family of four would drop $20 a visit.

With that knowledge in mind, the client and I headed upstairs to the boardwalk to employ a disarmingly simple leverage strategy, giving each retailer certificates worth 50¢ of free play that they could gift to anyone who made a purchase in their store, whether for a hot dog, balloon, kite, or pretzel on a stick. The retailers loved it, because it enticed customers to make a purchase at their business as well, and it didn't cost them a dime.

We limited the certificates to one per person, assuming that the statistical probability of a family using it was very high. At one certificate per person, with an average family spending $20, we estimated that we'd be attracting $18 worth of net business on every four we gave away. And that's exactly what we pulled in!

The data speak. They will tell you almost anything you want to know, but you have to know how to ask. The data will tell you where to put your money for long-term growth, or what sources are best if you need cash flow right now. They will also tell you how to strategically balance your activities both for the moment and for the future—but only if you analyze them.

KNOW YOUR BUSINESS'S *SYSTEM*, SO YOU CAN CONVERT AND MAINTAIN CLIENTS

We've talked about strategizing and analyzing; that leaves us with the final way to counteract unpredictable sales volume. None of this is possible unless you get your hands around what you're doing. And what you're doing means knowing what game you're playing long term. In other words, you need to know your system.

For most businesses, the long-term game should be targeting access to the best-quality clientele, which in turns leads to making the easiest proposition to get them to start a relationship with you right away. It can be a compensative relationship in which a transaction is made, or it can be a courting relationship whereby the prospect receives initial information or free goods, all geared to prep her for the imminent first sale.

Your goal is then to convert that to the first-time sale. Usually, but not always, your first-time sale (or smaller-sized initial transaction) might be priced less because it's easier to move first-time buyers up over time—to more significant products or product-services combinations—down the road, once you've established a bonded/trusted relationship. Once you've moved them forward and upward, you want to keep doing it over and over again.

Keep in mind that the hardest part of client relationships is bringing in buyers for the first time. It's far easier to sell to them a second time than it was at first, if you have strategic control of the selling situation. Either *it* controls you, or *you* control it. Unfortunately, in 95 percent of the cases, the latter occurs. Don't let that happen to your business!

You need a dynamic system to convert and maintain clients, and your old one probably won't do. The second-biggest mistake made by small- to medium-sized businesses—after failing to be strategic, analytical, and systemic—is to apply a one-size-fits-all approach to their client base and economic business growth model.

You can't afford to make that mistake. Some prospects merit less time or attention than others. The Pareto Principle (sometimes also referred to as the 80–20 Rule or the Rule of the Vital Few) states that 20 percent of your client base will be worth 80 percent of your profits, and 20 percent of your client base will be the cause of 80 percent of your headaches. Clearly, the 20 percent of your clients who are worth 80 percent of your profits deserve far more time and attention (and financial investment) than the flagging 80 percent of your clients who produce only 20 percent of your profits.

But you can't focus on your best 20 percent *if you don't know who they are*. And you won't find them if you don't know how to analyze and correlate what the data are showing. Analyzing and systemizing go hand in hand; you can't have one without the other.

There are a lot of procedures that can help you with data analysis, but to start, look at your buyer base. Locate your prospect base. Ask yourself what you know about the cost of a prospect based on its source. Because rarely are two different prospects worth the same amount. A referral, for example, is the result of an established relationship with one of your best current clients, and therefore will likely be far more valuable than a prospect who comes in blind from the Yellow Pages or a newspaper ad. However, that can vary based on the company and business you're in. It's up to you to analyze your data, discover the cost and worth of each of your different prospects and clients, and then engineer a system that maximizes the long-term value of whatever you've learned.

Ask yourself what you know about categories of leads, how they convert, and what different products/services they convert for. Usually there will be a predictable correlation to the lion's share of transactions and profits. Try to retroactively analyze the origin of your clients, then project conservatively

- what specifically they will most likely buy in the future,

- how often they will buy,

- and how long they will continue to buy.

Knowing those three details will help you analyze each client's short- and long-term worth to you, and, by extension, which categories are worth more than others. Let's look at an example.

Suppose you have a mail-order company, and your tool buyers tend to be repeat buyers, whereas buyers of faddish yet more expensive electronics tend to be one-time shoppers.

Even though the electronic fad buyer is worth more initially, the tool buyer is more profitable to you over time. That's not to say that you want to drop the former; it might be good to have some of these fad buyers in your strategy to momentarily stimulate positive, short-term cash flow while you're building the other long-term, back-end categories of business—the predictable repeat buyers.

Similarly, when I was in the subscription-based newsletter and magazine business, my associates and I had formulas that could predict with reasonable accuracy (based on the people who came in from a different type of promotion) what our cash flow would be for the next two years if we kept up the same performance dynamic. There was a historic knowledge of what renewals and ancillary products/sales were worth and for how long. We had been doing the same business for so long that the connected dots were easy to see and project out. I call this "making the money connection."

Sometimes that first sale will open up a host of new opportunities in ways much different than you imagined. It might even forge a relationship that can be used for leveraging. Here's another example.

A few years ago, one of my clients published a magazine that was Number 3 in the travel market. The magazine sold ad space for $10,000 a pop, and that space cost the magazine only $1,000. But because nobody was buying the ads, the magazine was struggling. I went in to analyze my client's data and to look at the available options. Not surprisingly, the magazine was suffering because it didn't have a long-term strategy; it hadn't come up with a systemic way of dealing with the unpredictable nature of selling ads.

As it turned out, several people had offered to barter for ad space. But the magazine's execs didn't know what to do with barters, so they never took trades—or, rather, never took trades until I got there. By creating a system that would allow for barter, my associates and I were able to convert those ads to cash at 50¢ on the dollar, which was five times what their cost was. It was a nonlinear way to turn the ad pages into a monster profit center. (Chapter 6 covers bartering in more detail.)

Think of linear as the status quo. For example, if I'm in the advertising business and I sell advertising and get paid for it, that's what I call *linear*. This magazine had been doing things *linearly*, but it wasn't selling enough ads and its selling was highly erratic. So we looked at a *non*linear solution, which in this case happened to be bartering. And suddenly, the magazine was able to trade ad space for goods or services worth $10,000 a page. We had no trouble finding individuals and companies who were happy to pay 50¢ on the dollar—after all, this was the Number 3 magazine in the travel market. Meanwhile, the ad page cost the company only $1 on the dollar. Previously, it wasn't selling many ads at $10 on the dollar and was going negative. Yet now it was getting $5,000 cash for $10,000 pages, all day long.

Also, this magazine happened to be a quarterly. This meant that when and if it *did* sell advertising, the client would buy it, wait until it came out three months later, and then typically wait another sixty days to pay for it. So when the magazine started trading for ad space, it would get cash for the ad *five months earlier.* It was a win-win situation all around—and all it took was a little systematic thinking.

IT'S ALL IN THE NUMBERS:
KNOW WHERE YOUR HIGHEST REVENUE COMES FROM

If you truly want to get unstuck and improve not just a little but exponentially, you can't do it just with luck. The easiest way to ensure positive, profitable forward movement amidst an uncertain environment is to let the power of science and mathematics work together to your advantage. It's all in the numbers. Strategy and quantification will help you develop theories from your data. And testing involves taking these interpretive assumptions and trying them out empirically in the marketplace. Here's an example.

A few years ago, I worked with a small company in Texas that provided heating/air conditioning services. The owners and I did a thorough analysis of its metrics and determined that the majority of its business was driven by people who hired the company to come out and simply check up on their equipment. Out of every 100 furnaces or air conditioning units, it turned out that 80 needed work done—a solid 80 percent.

This company, however, had never assessed its numbers in a strategic way. Once the owners consciously confronted the statistics, they recognized a gold mine of opportunity. I worked with them to create a new service that we called a "tune-up and seasonal readiness package" and offered it twice yearly, once in winter and once in summer, for only $19. The company lost $10 to $15 on that deal because it paid the technician $30, but on the backend it made an average of $800 per call.

With this new strategy in place, the company offered its seasonal package twice a year, and that package spawned almost all of the company's business. This company had moved from the realm of guesswork and uncertainty to a strategic position where it was making lucrative sales on a regular basis—all because we'd taken time to go over the numbers.

There's another valid lesson in this story: Sometimes you have to start small and move up. The $19 readiness package described above was a great idea; the company owners found that it was much easier to initially pitch a $19 tune-up than $800 worth of repair work that would need to be done down the road. Here's how that lesson applies to another business— the bicycle business I mentioned earlier, which discovered that it was selling lots of bikes to doctors.

Suppose you're the owner of this bicycle business, and you want to target doctors for your new super-ergonomic racing bicycles, because a large number of doctors have already purchased a large percentage of your stock. The ergonomic bike sells for $6,000. It's possible that trying to sell that bike out of the gate is too high a sales hurdle, even when you're selling to doctors. So you decide to start off with a promotion for a lesser-priced, yet still hip, bike that's congruent with the ergonomic theme, then try to move the buyers up once the bikes are in the store, using the strategy of preeminence we explored in Chapter 2.

As the doctor stands eyeing the lesser-priced model, you say: "You're obviously a serious road-bike aficionado. And this is a great bike for most people, but frankly, I think you should look at our super-colossal ergonomic model, because we sell more of those to doctors such as yourself than to anyone else in town. Take a test-ride around the block and see the difference for yourself. Oh, and we have a great financing package."

In reality, you should test both strategies—both marketing the high-end bicycles up front and starting with the lower-end model to graduate the sale, because there's no way of knowing for certain what the market will best respond to. Either it'll work or it won't. Or perhaps it will work better than the way you've been doing it, or work less well. Very rarely will these two options have the same effect. If it works less well, then you're most likely wrong in your assumptions. If it works better, it means you should probably replace your old process with the newly tested one. Either way, you'll know quickly and definitively which action to take for maximum results.

But if that happens, don't stop there. Your goal is to keep testing, then uncovering bigger and better performing systems and strategies based on "following the evidence" (or data, in this case), as Gil Grissom says on *CSI*.

That's what I mean by being strategic. It means moving from the attitude of "getting through the month" and then having to start all over again, from zero, on the first of the next month. There's already enough uncertainty in the surrounding world—it doesn't have to define your business volume as well. Be proactive about finding ways to garner steady sales, even when times are tenuous. Recall our earlier examples: Colonial Penn creating AARP to exponentially increase its sales; the travel magazine figuring out how to barter for ad space; the initiative launched to sell ergonomic bicycles to doctors who just love to ride. The recommendation implicit in all three is that you should move toward an approach that smooths out your erratic business volume and instead gives you long-term certainty about the profitability of your business—while also building the confidence you need to take your business to the next level and beyond. With a predictable, sustainable revenue-generating system in place, you can be certain that profits and clients will flow to your business for years to come.

Now it's time to take our discussion on strategizing to the next level, too.

The Bottom Line

■ To smooth out your erratic business volume, you have to start acting strategically, analytically, and systematically.

- Take only those actions that *always* advance and enhance your long-term strategy of attracting prospects, converting them to clients, and creating a lasting, repeat-buying relationship with them.

- The most important step in strategizing is to ask yourself: What kind of people or businesses do you want your business to attract, and why? Do marketplace research to answer this question.

- Analyze your past and current actions. Quantification analysis is the only way to determine how to invest with the optimal long-term, financial, and strategic business return in mind.

- Twenty percent of your clients are worth 80 percent of your profits. Find out who they are and what they want—then give it to them.

- Create a system for converting and maintaining clients. Constantly return to analyzing so as to test and perfect your system.

☞ **Immediate Action Step** Take out a sheet of paper and define your ideal client or prospect by answering these questions:

1. What problem does your ideal client have that you can solve effectively and profitably?
2. What kind of individual or company is your ideal client? Where is it located, how big is it, and why do you enjoy serving it?

It's a little like making a list of the characteristics you seek in a spouse or partner! By committing these thoughts to paper, you attract (to use the buzzword of the day) these people or companies to you—and you stop chasing revenue sources that don't make your business stronger (such as people who will nickel-and-dime you, but you go after them anyway because they're waving a credit card at you).

Keep this definition of your ideal client where everyone in your organization can see it every day.

5

ARE YOU STUCK FAILING TO STRATEGIZE?

If the typical businessperson were to keep a diary for one month of all her business activities, she would likely discover up to 80 percent of those activities to be nonproductive and diversionary. Most businesspeople fail to focus on managing, strategizing, and working on higher-performing, constant-growth issues. They just keep on spending time, money, and human capital the way they've always spent it, and they achieve the expected plateau-causing results. But other businesspeople are *strategic*; here's an example.

One of my former clients, "Sam," owned a medical delivery service, and each morning, Sam's deliverymen would rush to pick up blood and vital organs for transplants, then hurry their precious cargo to doctors in various medical labs and hospitals around the city. Because they were delivering blood and other perishable items, time was of the essence. On the way back from these deliveries, however, the trucks were deadheaded: Half the time the vehicles were on the road, they were empty, and they weren't making any profit. As a result, the business overall was only marginally profitable.

Until one day when all that changed. Why? Because Sam started strategizing.

Sam came up with a brilliant plan: He realized that he could pick up deliveries that were not time-critical on the way *back* from deliveries that were. Because this strategy required leveraging, Sam approached other people to launch his plan into action. One of the businesses he approached was a small-package delivery service that was struggling to pay staff and processing fees.

Sam made the owner of this business a simple proposition. "What if I give you the opportunity to eliminate all of your staff and processing fees," he said, "and split revenue with me instead? Your deliveries will be guaranteed in four hours—probably much less." Not surprisingly, the business owner, who dealt in noncritical deliveries, jumped at the deal.

With this new strategy in place, all of the deliveries Sam's employees made on the journey back earned a profit. Thus he was able to double his profits with no further investment, turning his marginal delivery service into a lucrative business. And he helped out the other company, too.

If you're failing to strategize, you're probably using your time in the wrong ways. Just as Sam's delivery trucks were empty and deadheaded half the time, you, too, may be harnessing your time and resources ineffectively 50 or more percent of the time. In this chapter, I'll show you the secret to managing your time and talents. It begins with what I like to call the "highest and best use" concept, a theory of true time management.

Most businesspeople fail to view time expenditure the same way they view all other expenditures in their lives—even though *time* is one of the three most precious, intangible assets they possess. (The other two are *energy* and *opportunity costs*.) Indeed, they waste time on unimportant things when they could be investing it in their strategy. As a result, they miss out on valuable opportunities to grow and expand their business. Most people just don't make the highest and best use of what they've got. Fortunately, you no longer have to count yourself among their ranks.

Everybody knows at least one highly productive person, someone for whom there seems to be more than twenty-four hours in a day. This person is ten times more productive than her competitor because she understands the concept of highest and best use. It's a rather simple—yet inarguable—concept: Use your time to produce the greatest strategic, long-term pay-off. It's that simple.

So, let's talk about how to optimize the highest and best use not just of your time but also of your relationships, opportunities, activities, and expenses.

THE SECRET OF THE HIGHEST AND BEST USE OF YOUR TIME AND TALENTS

The concept of highest and best use is deceptively easy. Just use your time and your talents to the maximum potential—simple, right?

And yet, most of the business world fails to do it. If you're not practicing the concept of highest and best use, you're sacrificing your potential, your profits, and your future. For starters, most people don't have a clue as to which items on their to-do list actually qualify as "highest" and "best." If you're thinking to yourself, "Hmmm. I'm not sure I do, either," you might be working at a *third* or less of your capacity, because you're spending time on tasks that are far less important or result in much smaller payoff than those you could be doing. That's a lot of efficiency you can't stand to lose!

Let's try an exercise right now that will help you identify your "highest" and "best." Start by writing down the three most critical tasks you're paid by your business to do. Then break those three tasks down into sub-tasks, for which there are usually as many as seven. Finally, give each of those sub-tasks three different values based on their *relevancy*, your *competency*, and your true *passion* for doing them.

Now it's time to review what you've come up with. If the task is not relevant but you're competent at it, it's a waste of your time. If your competency in a particular task is less than average, then you're not the most efficient person for the job, which means it's a huge expenditure of energy and, again, a waste of your time. For example, why should you review every employee's time card if doing so eats up half your day? My point is not that the time cards shouldn't be reviewed but, rather, that *you* shouldn't be the one reviewing them. Get someone else to do this task, then spot-check or audit his or her work.

What this exercise will help you do is determine which tasks you should permanently remove from your to-do list, so that you can put yourself into the power position that brings the greatest yield. Whatever your tasks and subtasks may be, it's imperative that you work on the tasks that are most important for *you*. Here's the bottom line:

Anything that isn't relevant, that you're not competent in, or that you're not completely passionate about should be delegated to somebody else.

This is true even if it means you need ten people doing the same job 80 percent as well as you. That still amounts to eight times greater efficiency and results than would be the case if you did 100 percent of the job yourself. It frees you up to focus your most precious assets—your time, energy, and opportunity costs—on the things that matter most and that deliver the most meaningful ongoing results.

The Fine Art of Delegation

So let's assume you've come up with a list of tasks, a few of which could easily stand to be nixed from your to-do list. But they have to be done by *someone*, right? That brings us to our next point of discussion: delegation.

The best way to delegate is to give what you consider work to people who think it's play. A task that makes you cringe may be just the sort of job someone else looks forward to most. It sounds crazy, I know—but it works. Let's look at an example.

Suppose one of your least favorite activities is talking on the phone. Cold-calling prospects is a dreaded task for you, but one that nonetheless needs to be completed. What do you do? You find someone who has no problem talking to strangers and who spends so much time on the phone, you'd think it was glued to his ear. To him, there are much worse tasks he could be given than picking up the phone and chatting up someone new. He loves the challenge! So while your new salesperson is busy knocking names off his prospect list, you can focus on a job for which you have true competency, relevancy, and passion.

In my own business, I have an intern—we pay him, but he's not as expensive as a full-time employee—who handles the trivial tasks that would otherwise devour my time. He waits in line to purchase my iPhone, then he sets it up. He researches the best hands-free earpiece and then buys it. And he actually *enjoys* these tasks. If I were to do them myself, they'd eat up three hours of my day—three hours away from my time spent focusing on highest and best use, which is making people like you a lot more money. Ask yourself: What is your time currently worth? What do you *want* it to be worth?

Here's another example:

A few years back, I was in the United Kingdom at a conference attended by some of the most prominent members of the business community, including one businessman who was in *The Guinness Book of World Records* for selling the most merchandise per square foot in Europe. Upon learning that every executive on this businessman's staff was chauffeured around in luxury automobiles, one of the other attendees accused him of being arrogant and materialistic for indulging in such an extravagance.

The businessman didn't flinch. "Is your time," he asked the man, "worth more than seven pounds an hour? I know that for me, my commute time is better spent focusing and strategizing rather than concentrating on traffic lights and avoiding pedestrians. I'm not really paying seven pounds to be driven to work. I'm paying seven pounds to claim two priceless hours of my life back, two hours each day, which I'll use to expand my business many times over. I don't see those seven pounds as an expense; I see them as an investment, paying Herculean returns. It's impossible to fathom their value."

When I make this argument to my own clients, many of them tell me, "But, Jay, I can't afford to do that." To which I reply, "Wrong. You can't afford *not* to."

If you don't have the money to hire assistants the traditional way, you can employ the concept of leveraging that we explored briefly in Chapter 3 and will look at in depth in Chapter 10. When you bring leveraging into the equation, you create exponential options and opportunities. Let's consider the example of an administrative assistant.

Every major city in the world is brimming with underutilized administrative assistants—those on maternity leave, those who have retired, and, of course, those who aren't working full-time or at all at the moment. Even if you can't pay them with a traditional paycheck, you have many options. You can compensate them through a deferred salary that is quantifiable based on the company's productivity that they helped you achieve. For example, as the company makes 10 percent more in profits, each of these employees receives a defined percentage of that amount or a pre-set bonus.

Alternatively, you can offer to pay them only after the business makes a specified minimum benchmark amount more, at which point they receive a regular salary, plus a bonus. Yet another way is to tie their compensation to a quantifiable measurement such as a reduction in overhead expenses or an increase in sales. Or do it the old-fashioned way: by bartering or trading. The number of ways you can compensate these administrative assistants when your business doesn't have the cash to pay them a traditional wage is limited only by your imagination.

Usually when people claim to have "tried it all," they haven't. They're stuck thinking within the same old mindset. And I've seen this revealed—firsthand.

At a Tony Robbins seminar I once attended, a man came up on stage, in front of thousands of people, and asked for advice. "Tony, I've tried *everything* to make more money. I can't do it."

Tony was skeptical. "Name the last twenty-five to thirty new tactics you've tried in the last six or seven months and describe how each performed."

The man was speechless. He couldn't name a single one. Tony didn't give up. "Okay, name just ten." The man could only mutter unintelligibly before Tony finally drove the point home: "Just what *have* you done?"

The man's response shocked me: "I've looked in the want ads, and I've gone to a few franchise shows." Those two attempts hardly amounted to the "everything" he claimed to have tried. With his creative process stuck, the man was simply unable to see beyond the traditional methods he knew.

Are there times when you say you can't do something? If so, list the various methods you've already tried. Then see if you can list the spectrum of alternative options, opportunities, and possibilities you haven't even targeted. In doing so, you'll not only discover just how few methods you've actually attempted, but you may also see a pattern that helps you come up with a new angle to better your business philosophy.

The old axiom is true. There are indeed three kinds of people in the business world:

- People who make things happen.

- People who watch things happen.

- And people to whom things always seem to happen.

I honestly believe that people are where they are in life because that's ultimately where they want to be. Because if you didn't want to be there, you'd find an alternative. It isn't that hard. You just have to be willing to work at opening your mind to higher and better practices and pathways to pursue.

Schedule All E-Mails, Phone Calls, and Meetings— So You Choose When to Handle Them

I may not make any friends with the following statement, but I'll stand by it: What most people view as one of the most efficient technological breakthroughs in the history of business is actually one of the biggest wastes of time. E-mail may seem to be a blessing, but it's a curse when it comes to time management. The very feature that most people believe is so revolutionary— e-mail's immediacy—is what makes it so downright insidious: Nobody schedules time for it.

Replying to e-mail is a *task*, and as with any other task, you should schedule time for completing it. But most people e-mail continuously throughout the day. It doesn't matter if they're in the middle of a critical project or if an incoming message has little or no relevancy. All they need to hear is that delicate ping from their inbox, and they drop what they're doing to heed the call. What so many people view as instantaneous and constant access is actually instantaneous and constant diversion and distraction. It is time wastage—the lowest and worst use of your time.

I look at my e-mail only two times a day—and when I do so, it's already been sorted and prioritized for me. If a particular message is urgent, my assistant will interrupt me and let me know. Rather than being tied to the computer, I'm free to concentrate on the highest and best use of my time, thereby ensuring that I'm performing at my optimum.

There's an unrealistic expectation that as soon as an e-mail is received, the recipient will respond. There's no law that says you have to respond to e-mail—ever. You will not be arrested. The message will not self-destruct—you're not living out a scene from *Mission Impossible*. As I pointed out in Chapter 4, some prospects merit less time or attention than others; the same is true of communications. If I had to guess, I'd say that 80 percent of business e-mails are of low priority. Yet most people tend to treat e-mails with equal importance, as if these messages are bestowed with great significance simply by virtue of having been delivered electronically. It just isn't so.

Much of this reaction can be attributed to fear—fear that we might miss an important message or deal. It's as if people are caught up in a Pavlovian reaction initiated by the sound of new messages arriving: When they hear the ping, they're propelled into action, as if by the start of a race gun. But instantaneous reaction is not the highest and best use of their time. Thinking and reflecting would allow for a much more conscientious and astute response—something lacking in electronic communication in the vast majority of cases.

Today, it's also very easy to misjudge or to be misjudged in e-mail communications because the medium doesn't allow for tone, inflection, and emotional pitch. But that can be avoided if you allow for reflection. Take your time—both in reading and responding to your e-mail. After all, you're not Batman responding to the Bat Signal to save Gotham City!

The businesspeople I admire most are those who schedule specific times for phone calls and meetings. The rest of their day is spent focusing on productive growth-generating activities. In some instances, even those who work for someone else manage to incorporate this time-saving strategy into their workplace. The most productive people of all also require that every meeting have an agenda, which includes a summary of what the meeting's about, the expected outcome, the topics of discussion and how much time is allotted to each, and the priorities involved. In short, they, like any winning team, have a game plan—and they follow it.

If you work for someone else, suggest that office meetings have agendas, or take the lead and create the agendas yourself. The time you spend doing so will be repaid many times over with more productive, efficient meetings. Once the others in your office get hooked on these meeting agendas and come to expect them, delegate the task to someone else. In today's ultra-competitive world, it's important to be as efficient as possible. Moreover, if you can be diplomatic in making your suggestion or in setting an example, both your manager and your co-workers will appreciate the organization you bring to the process. Organization turns chaos into structure. And structure breeds strategy.

Work on Your Business, Not in Your Business

Why should you work on your business instead of in it? That's easy: because you want your business working harder for you than you work for it.

It's amazing what a difference a preposition can make. The significance of working *in* your business versus working *on* your business is enormous. Working *in* the business means you're just managing to accomplish the bare-minimum tasks that will get your rent paid and keep your company around to see the next day. You're answering e-mails, scrambling for clients, and making sure your office electricity bill is paid for the month so that you're not making cold-calls in the dark.

Working *on* the business, by contrast, means being strategic enough that you're involved in activities that will not only maintain but also grow your business—for tomorrow and beyond. Generating such a strategy requires very deep, concentrated thinking, which deserves more of your time, attention, and even respect than any other activity. When you work *on* the business, you must break it down into its key functions—

strategy, marketing, innovation, management, and so on—which you then allocate as the highest and best use of time, either yours or another employee's. In short, your job is to work on the biggest moneymakers, not on the biggest time-, energy-, and opportunity-drainers.

To help you identify the biggest moneymakers, I've provided below a list of eleven strategic pillars that any business truly implementing highest-and-best-use principles rests upon and grows from. These are the keys to working *on* your business. They aren't steps you'll implement one time and move forward from; rather, they're tools that you'll continuously utilize to ensure that your business is always working for you.

Eleven Keys to Working on Your Business

1. Continue to identify and discover hidden assets in your business.

2. Mine cash windfalls out of your business each and every month.

3. Engineer success into every action you take or decision you make.

4. Build your business on a foundation of multiple profit sources instead of depending on a single revenue source.

5. Be different, unique, and advantageous in the eyes of your clients.

6. For maximum loyalty and results, create real value for your clients and employees.

7. Gain the maximum personal leverage from every action, investment, and time or energy commitment you ever make.

8. Network/mastermind/brainstorm with like-minded, success-driven people who share real-life experiences with you.

9. Turn yourself into an idea-generator and recognized innovator within your industry or market.

10. Make "growth-thinking" a natural part of your everyday business philosophy.

11. Reverse the risk both for yourself and for your clients in everything you do (so the downside is almost zero, and the upside potential nearly infinite).

If there are items on your personal task list that don't correspond to one or more of these eleven keys, take them off—or, if really necessary to your business, delegate them. But devote yourself to the highest and best principles, without dilution or distraction. This will ensure the maximum potency when it comes to your ability to strategize. Here's a great example.

One of my former clients was a man named Patrick Flanagan who sold telephone systems. He got most of his business through cold-calling, which was an ineffective (not to mention frustrating) method. There wasn't much of a strategy underlying Patrick's actions.

Patrick sold systems for a major firm whose clients fell into two distinct groups: corporate clients and small-business clients. Patrick, though, had the right to sell only to the small businesses. On the other hand, he didn't have territorial restrictions, and as he plotted out how to implement his new strategy, he used that fact to full advantage.

Patrick's plan was simple: He would go to all of his manufacturers—the large-firm ones—and ask to buy all their rejects (i.e., the phone systems that were too small for them). Then he'd sell those to his client base (the small businesses) and give the large manufacturers a share of the profits.

Did it work? You bet it worked. Patrick Flanagan built a multimillion-dollar company simply by changing his strategy. By focusing on the things that mattered, he experienced an unprecedented level of success.

Don't Be Afraid of Change

Sometimes creating a brilliant strategy requires that you change the way you do things. Again, it's a lesson from the Indiana Jones School of Business:

> *When things aren't working,*
> *change your tactics.*

Let's say that you've now mastered time management. You've hired an assistant to manage your e-mails and are focusing on the twelve strategic tools needed to take your business in a new direction. You've laid all the groundwork. There's only one last thing you need before launching a world-class strategy: a reality check.

People are suffering right now. Whether or not you're paying them the same salary or hourly rate as before, your employees are hurting. They're struggling with the economy and rising costs, just as you are. Your buyers are hurting as well, either because their businesses, employers, or incomes are down or because there have been cutbacks at their own offices.

Here's a sobering fact: In today's volatile market, 80 percent of businesses are struggling, and the small ones are not growing. In fact, most of them are regressing. Employees are psychologically debilitated by the daily-grind factors, like watching their 401(k)s disappear or seeing their benefits cut and their salaries reduced (or, at best, capped).

You can see all of this turmoil at your own place of business. Know, too, that it is happening at other businesses, most likely the ones where your clients and prospects work. Having a respectful appreciation of this situation and a heartfelt desire to make your clients' lives better, richer, easier, and safer can actually improve your own bottom line. In such a brutal climate, your decision to stand out can make the difference in your business's survival. Why? Because you invest more in the buying and post-purchase experiences of your clients. You focus more attention on the issues most critically important to them, you address and fulfill more of the value that they appreciate, and you channel empathy into all interactions.

The starting point for empathy is to always remain positive and pleasant when interacting with a client or prospect. That may seem almost offensively obvious, but it's hard to maintain confidence, certainty, and enthusiasm for the buyer's outcome when your business is struggling and you are stressing. Empathy is the cornerstone of any effective business strategy. Put simply, you have to fall in love with the client.

What's it like when you're in love? The object of your affection basically becomes the center of your whole world. Everything else fades into the distance, and you live, breathe, and dream for that one special somebody.

Your relationship with your clients has to be similar to this. They become your almost all-consuming focus. That makes it easy for you to be exceedingly hopeful and encouraging in their behalf, because your job will be to help them engineer a better outcome from each transaction with you. You must make a conscious decision to make their lives better off as a result of your interchange.

You can do this by demonstrating how much more you understand, respect, are invested in, and empathize with their circumstances. Repeat back to them what you hear the clients expressing; put their problems and feelings into words so that you can be sure you understand the specific needs you've been called on to address. It's the first lesson in Empathy 101:

Show that you feel what your clients feel.

Don't worry: You don't need to enroll in acting courses to do this. If you recognize that your success and the client's are one and the same, empathetically engaging will occur so effortlessly that you'll forget it's a component of your business strategy. It will simply become second nature—part of who you are as a person, not just as a businessperson.

This shift in personality, focus, and interest matters now for two reasons:

- First, people need to feel valued and appreciated— and to genuinely *be* valued and appreciated.

- Second, all your competitors are struggling, so they're going to cut corners, get more irritable, and become internally focused on their own survival. As a result, they will compromise on sensitivity and their connectivity to the market. You *must not* do the same.

You have to be a source of stability in times of instability. Yes, your business has to make changes, too; it must evolve and grow. But in the meantime you have to provide the stability that people in need can turn to, trust in, and come back to again and again. Here's an example.

There was a builder in Australia who specialized in first-time home buyers. He was spending $10,000 to $15,000 per sale to attract buyers. After attending one of my long programs, he realized that the major pool of first-time buyers was made up of people currently living in apartment buildings. So, he went to apartment-building owners and got them to offer their renters his homes as a logical next step forward in their lives.

Obviously, the apartments weren't going to offer up perfectly good clients if they didn't stand to gain something, too. So the builder rewarded the apartment building owners for sending clients his way: Anyone who moved out of his or her apartment and into one of his homes earned the owner $5,000. And my builder went a step further: He agreed to underwrite, for up to a year, any unrented apartment vacated by someone buying his homes. At about $500 a month for the apartments he was targeting, that amounted to $6,000 a year. His maximum investment in each sale, then, was $11,000—$4,000 less than he was spending before.

What happened? He not only sold millions and millions of dollars' worth of homes but did so in a way that helped first-time home buyers make that big, scary first step, eliminated the risk of leaving their apartments behind, and netted the apartment building owners a handsome profit on the deal. He turned his selling strategy from a *self-focused* campaign that was only draining his coffers to a *client-focused, problem-solving* campaign. That made him millions.

When you have the courage to change your sales strategy and tactics, three important things will happen:

1. You'll close a lot more prospects than you used to, and you'll increase productivity and transaction size—which in turn translate into profitability— from the same time and effort.

2. You'll influence a large number of people (and usually the best people, because they'll have a higher-level appreciation for what you're doing) as a result of having created a discernible distance between yourself and your competitors.

3. You'll get the lion's share of new people coming into the market because you'll stand out as the most appealing choice anyone could possibly make.

These three things will happen almost spontaneously if you just get yourself in philosophical alignment. It's always about *them*, your buyers or your prospects. It's never about *you*, the seller. Keep that in mind, and your strategy will start to crystallize.

THE POWER OF THE THREE P'S: YOUR BUSINESS'S PURPOSE, POSSIBILITY, AND PASSION

Earlier in the chapter, I mentioned that you should grade your tasks based on three criteria: relevancy, competency, and passion. The success of your business itself is based on three similar factors: purpose, possibility, and, again, passion. These three P's should form the crux of your business strategy.

The Power of Purpose

Purpose refers not just to the market niche your product or service fills but to the greater good you bring to that marketplace. For instance, your widget factory may be active not just in the business world but also in the community, by sponsoring a Little League team, say, or adopting a highway. Of course, a business can run—even thrive—without a philanthropic purpose. But the benefits from working for a larger cause stretch far beyond improved community reputation, ultimately encompassing improvements in morale, both your own and your staff's. When your business has a higher purpose, you never have to question why you go to work each day. The evidence stares you right in the face.

Frankly, the greatest causal purpose your business could ever strive for is to contribute more value, benefits, advantages, and worth to your buyers with respect to what you sell and how that product or service performs for them. If you want to discover your purpose—in terms of both your market niche and a higher cause—you have to identify *what your business does* (or can start doing) *better than anyone else*. After all, when someone buys from you, they're choosing to do so over three other options:

- They're buying from you instead of buying from your competition.

- They're buying from you instead of choosing an alternative form of solving their problem or fulfilling their opportunity (e.g., using a hand-cranking can opener rather than buying your electric one).

- They're buying from you instead of doing absolutely nothing.

Whichever option applies to a given situation, it's imperative that you acknowledge the *real* reason why clients should buy from you. Ultimately, that reason has to be a benefit for *them*, not for your bank account.

The Power of Possibility

The second ingredient for a thriving business is *possibility*. Without possibility, you have no potential, no vision. And without vision, there is no innovation, which is the key to all growth. Exercising your possibility is much like going to the gym. If you perform the same exercises all the time, eventually you'll stop seeing results. You have to innovate and find fresh ways to challenge your muscles so they'll continue to develop. It's no different with your business.

Start thinking about possibility multi-dimensionally. For example, consider the following four angles from which to launch yourself into a world of potential:

- You could envision *bigger* possibility in terms of what you can add to the client's buying experience.

- Or you might visualize ways to *broaden* possibility with respect to what your business can grow to be-

come, where your business can extend its relationships, and how many more ways it can sell and
market.

■ You could create plans for *longer-reaching* possibility in all the meaningful things you and your business can do with a portion of your increased profits.

■ And don't forget the element of *time:* Plan out the
future and think of ways your business can impact
the world yet to come.

The Power of Passion

The third vital ingredient for your business is *passion*. Passion is
the fuel that drives all achievement, whether in art, technology,
or marriage. You can't underestimate its power as the driving
force behind your business. Your passion has to be a love not
just for the business itself but for the marketplace your business
affects. I'm referring here not just to the industry you're in but
also to the purpose your business serves in the community and
to the enrichment of the lives of the people you work with. Find
your passion, and possibility and purpose won't be far behind.

Think of the 3 P's as the wheels to your business strategy:
They set your dreams in motion. And as for the "highest and
best use" of time and resource management: Think of these as
your pre-trip checklist and the highway gas stations where you
check in along the way. Put them all together and, just like
Sam's medical delivery service, which I described at the beginning of this chapter, you're on the road to a prosperous future
in the land of milk and profit.

Now it's time to face the next challenge: what to do when
insidious costs linger like ravenous wolves, threatening to en-
croach on your blissful profit paradise.

The Bottom Line

- Strategizing begins with true time management—putting everything you do to the "highest and best use" test.

- *Time*, *energy*, and *opportunity costs* are the three most valuable intangible assets you have. Don't waste any of these when you could be investing them in your strategy.

- Evaluate all of your tasks. Anything that isn't *relevant*, that you're not *competent* in, or that you're not completely *passionate* about should be delegated to somebody else.

- Delegation means giving what you consider work to people who think it's play.

- If you can't afford to pay assistants and employees in the traditional ways, find creative ways to compensate them.

- Schedule specific and limited time for e-mails, phone calls, and meetings. Don't let them take over your calendar.

- Create agendas for office meetings and stick to them.

- Take action on the "Eleven Keys to Working *on* Your Business"; don't be a hamster on a wheel, working *in* your business.

- Your success and the success of your clients are one and the same. Show them that you feel what they feel.

- Know your *purpose*. What is the greater good that you bring to the marketplace?

■ Think of *possibility* multi-dimensionally. How can you create bigger, broader, longer-reaching, and longer-lasting possibility?

■ Love your business, and the marketplace it affects, with a *passion*.

☞ **Immediate Action Step** Stop being your own administrative assistant. Develop the discipline to delegate, and start by having someone else read your e-mail for you. Clients aren't paying you to read your own e-mail. They're paying you to solve problems, so devote more of your time to the actions that actually generate revenue. Your time is too valuable to squander on anything else.

6

ARE YOU STUCK WITH COSTS EATING UP ALL YOUR PROFITS?

When I was growing up, I loved to eavesdrop on the conversations my mother had with her friends. They'd sit on our back porch, sipping lemonade and chatting about their kids. Sometimes—and always when she was talking about me, it seemed—my mother would press her lips together, shake her head, and say, "I declare, anything you tell that boy goes in one ear and out the other."

It's the perfect metaphor for what happens to so many businesses today. Except it's not words going in one way and out the other; it's cash flow. And whereas my leaky eardrums usually only got me scolded or sent to my room, the consequences of a leaky wallet can be disastrous for your business.

A good many stagnating businesses don't have a problem getting money to flow in—they just have a hard time preventing it from flowing right back out. It's as though the owners have holes in their pockets: Every penny they make seems to be gone before they know it. Overhead costs such as salaries, equipment, and infrastructure sap up the profits like a thirsty sponge.

If this sounds like your company, one of your main cash-flow sinkholes is probably that you haven't been measuring the return on investment (ROI) of your marketing. The second most important step is to adjust your measurement horizon in terms of your overall outlook, because if your business is declining rapidly, you can't operate as you did before. Finally, no matter how tempted you are to cut back on sales and marketing in times of strain, the opposite is actually what will save your skin.

In this chapter, we'll talk about all your cash-flow problems. I'll show you what to do if you have too much overhead; if you don't have enough overhead; if you don't have enough money to do the right things; and if you're not demanding the right performance from your investments. We'll examine all of these components in one chapter because they all relate to the problem of excess expenses cutting into your profits.

At some point in my personal development, I realized I should probably work on plugging up the leak between my ears that my mother had so keenly identified. I'm happy to say I did: I began listening to (and retaining) the messages that other people delivered. In other words, I grew up.

It's time for your business to grow up, too—in the sense that, if you break your bad cash-flow habits, you'll see a revolutionized profit margin in no time.

So let's get started plugging up those financial leaks.

RETURNING TO ROI: MEASURE EVERYTHING YOU DO

When the market starts to decline, the knee-jerk reaction of many businesspeople is to reduce their marketing budgets. But what they're really doing is reducing their investment in growing their business, so their cutbacks become a self-perpetuating downward spiral. Unfortunately, I see this time and again in stagnating businesses.

The vast majority of the time, I've found that my clients blindly put their faith in "revenue-generating activities" that barely—if at all—earn back their initial cost. But this fact often remains buried beneath piles of bills because so few people bother to measure the performance of their marketing activities. Each process must be broken down and analyzed for its effectiveness, a subject we touched upon in Chapter 4.

Any business that sells anybody anything has to first target the audience who will be the most responsive. You have to reach the audience, or motivate the audience to come to you. You then have to close the audience either on the transaction that brought them in or on a starter transaction that initiates a sustaining, recurring relationship that will continue to yield returns for both sides.

Each of the processes I just mentioned is a sub-element of generating and sustaining business. However, most companies don't measure the performance of these individual processes and so continue to spend money in nonperforming or underperforming areas. Remember the story in Chapter 4 about the client whose business was in bioidentical hormones? That company's managers almost stopped running highly profitable ads because they gravely miscalculated their ROI.

There are other return factors to consider when it comes to targeting your audience, like utilization of assets and utilization of workforce. You might be paying salaries to salespeople who aren't selling or aren't selling enough to justify your investment in them. Or you're running ads that aren't capturing viewers' attention or response. Or perhaps you're generating referrals that aren't being converted to sales. If the members of your sales team are making presentations and you're not monitoring how many they've made, what their closing rate is, what the average unit of sale is, what the profit on that sale is, and how much future profit results from those first-time buyers, then you're wasting a lot of money. No matter what the activity, if you're not quantifying its performance, you're not realizing its fullest potential.

Whereas some businesspeople shy away from marketing expenditures when they see the economy start to shift downward, others start frantically dumping more money into old practices, even though they've never measured the ROI of these activities. Obviously, doing more of what wasn't working during good times won't get you through an economically challenging period. When businesses are stuck or declining, it's even more important to analyze every activity in terms of how much you get back for every dollar you put in.

Everything you do should be measured in terms of either an investment or a profit center, as opposed to just a cost expense. If you continue to evaluate every activity with the goal of growing and sustaining your business in mind, you'll have the ability to utilize assets you've already invested in instead of having to downsize or outsource. These just might become leverageable assets you can use for joint ventures, which we'll talk about in the next section of this chapter.

Business owners who really want to get unstuck need to get excited. And there's nothing more exciting than realizing that whereas the ROI for the money and work you put into a stock may be 10 or 15 percent, the ROI for the money and work you put into improving a marketing technique could be 10 or 15 *hundred* percent. And what's more, the ROI you can get from forging strategic partnerships ("power partnerships," as I call them) could be incalculable, because your out-of-pocket expense is very low—maybe even zero—even though you're getting the value of hundreds of thousands or even millions of dollars through other people's facilities, equipment, goodwill, infrastructure, and intellectual capital. Now that's what I call a bargain.

■ ■ ■

THE BETTER BUSINESS BARTERS: TRADE WHAT YOU HAVE FOR WHATEVER YOU NEED

One of the most dynamic means of achieving a greater ROI is through bartering. I could talk about the beauty of bartering all day long. Bartering allows for that ever-elusive combination of positive elements where all parties walk away happy: You benefit, your partner benefits, and your client benefits, too. There's really no loss to anyone involved. And with the way our economy is going, I am more convinced than ever that bartering is fundamentally important to the future of business.

Remember the top travel magazine from Chapter 4 that revolutionized the way it did business by accepting barters for its ad space? Now you can experience the same degree of explosive success.

Following are seven bartering strategies that you and your business could implement immediately.

1. *Save cash on capital expenditures.* Say you're buying a computer. After you've negotiated the lowest price you can get, agree to it only if the seller will take a portion of that negotiated price in your product or service—ideally, 25 or 50 percent. What does that accomplish? It lowers the true cost to you of the computer by up to one-third, depending on what your margins are, and it buys you time on the bartered portion of the purchase because most people won't use your products or services right away, even though they're welcome to. You, on the other hand, get access to the computer right away, so you've actually deferred payment interest free at a discount for that period of time.

You can even trade a lesser dollar value of your more desirable goods, and for a higher markup. If you don't think this is feasible, here's a real-world example that may change your mind.

I've seen car dealers trade cars for two or three times their value in "soft dollar" services, which I explain below. Let's say a service provider wants to do the window cleaning for them—or *anything*, really, because car dealers spend tens of millions of dollars on services and on products. Why shouldn't they leverage that need to their advantage?

So let's say *you* want to get in on this dynamic. If a car dealer is willing to trade to you initially, you can get a car. Let's say your product is marked up five times. The car dealer marks his up twice. You get the car for twice, and sell it for less than the car dealer would. You get a profit on your services, and you get access to the car dealer as a client when the trade runs out.

Alternatively, you can pay your operating expenditures, even payroll, by converting them to a variable or soft contract with "soft dollars." This means that you could be low on cash, or even out of cash, and still continue to operate and prosper, and continue to employ critically needed personnel or service providers using barter as your means of commerce.

I've gotten lots of stuff done for me in this way. For three or four years, all of my decorating, furniture-purchasing, and house-painting goals were accomplished through barter. I'd give somebody my services at $5,000 an hour, and he would give me his. My wife has a Porsche convertible. It cost me a day and a half of my time in trade, brand new.

2. *Print your own currency or scrip, usable only at your place of business.* Your imagination is the only limit to the advantages that having your own legal tender can provide to your business. Here's just one thing to think about: Say there's something your company really needs or wants to acquire, but you can't afford it on a cash bank basis. Using your own currency, whereby the cost is based on the cost of supply in goods and services, and where you take delivery now but pay for it much, much later, you can afford to acquire all kinds of things.

There are times when you have to triangulate. You may not have something that is wanted by the business you're trying to hook, but you may be able to trade your product or service to a third company or individual who's got that hook; then you triangulate it. Here's how it works.

Say you issue a $5,000 credit to a printer. She gives you $5,000 worth of printing and delivers it immediately. You pay with your barter scrip or credits, and you allow the printer one to two years to use those credits with you. Until the printer actually uses those credits, you haven't paid out a thing, and because she probably will use only a portion of the credit with you at a time, its cost will easily be handled a little at a time incrementally. But a dollar paid in two years costs you a lot less than a dollar paid today.

3. *Keep in mind that your bartering partner may never cash in.* This point is not meant to be manipulative or unethical. It's just a truism reflecting "breakage," which represents the barter certificates that are never used. A certain percentage of all barter credits issued, if they have an expiration date (which I recommend), will not be used. Here's an example.

A major New Orleans hotel traded $125,000 worth of radio and TV time, and issued barter scrip in that amount, for use of the hotel's services, with a one-year expiration date. Right up front, the hotel got $125,000 in advertising at regular cash rates. This was advertising for which the hotel had been paying $125,000 in real cash in the past.

At the end of twelve months, an audit revealed that the TV and radio stations had redeemed only $35,000 worth of the barter scrip within the time limit. The hotel was ready to make good on its barter scrip—it was willing and able to. But the rest of the credits expired unused, so the cash cost of the hotel delivering $35,000 worth of rooms was only $5,000. The hotel had leveraged up $125,000 in advertising for $5,000 in hard dollars.

Note that this calculation doesn't take into consideration two other factors that, although often overlooked, are extremely significant:

- Statistically, $35,000 in room trade produced $17,500 in cash, food, beverage, and miscellaneous real sales, with gross profits in excess of $8,000 for the hotel. So the hotel actually got paid $3,000 net after all expenses were entered into the transaction.

■ All $35,000 worth of rooms were not used at one time. The room reservations were spread out over twelve months, meaning that the hotel got to pay the $5,000 over twelve months totally interest free. In essence, the hotel received $125,000 worth of advertising up front, and got paid to use it.

In light of the evidence, I think we can safely say that this barter was one of the best decisions the hotel ever made.

4. *Convert your bartered items into cash.* Many barter items can be sold or converted to cash at a fee well above the cost of acquiring them. And this happens not only with small businesses but with Fortune 500 companies, too. Here's just one example.

A few years back, a Spanish television network traded with Chrysler Corporation for 192 cars. The seven-station chain sold the cars to its employees at a 30 percent discount over what the cars normally stickered for. The employees were overjoyed because the most the dealer would have discounted them was 15 percent. The average value of each car was $10,000, and ultimately, the television network received from the sale more than $1,920,000 in real cash for unused airtime that cost it nothing. This was expiring time the stations weren't using—time that probably would have gone unused and, thus, would have produced zero revenue unless it was traded.

But the deal gets even better: The radio station traded 45 of these Chrysler cars to a television transmitter manufacturer, in exchange for a half-million dollars' worth of transmitter equipment, which permitted the radio station to open up a new full-power UHF station in San Francisco without using *any* cash. The ability to trade for this equipment sped up the timetable to get the San Francisco station on the air by more than one full year; it also enabled the station to operate in the beginning without draining all its limited cash. That radio station became a runaway success before any other Spanish station ever penetrated San Francisco. And the station was subsequently sold for $400 million—really, $400 million—even though, by itself, it was probably worth only $50 million.

5. *Create a barter profit center*. Some salespeople who are not effective in cash selling are extremely successful in bartering. So you might have a sleeper salesperson working for you whose sales will skyrocket and give you huge bonus margins on the products or services once he or she starts bartering. You trade your products or services at full rate, then turn right around and sell the merchandise for services you acquire to the open market, at a discount, under the going rate for the merchandise. Here's a cool example.

The Home Shopping Network, which is now a billion-dollar business, was actually conceived and started by the owner of a small-time radio station in Florida who was having difficulty making payroll. The owner traded 1,400 electric can openers (really!) with a hardware store and then cash-converted them over the air. Lo and behold, his company was saved. He basically held an auction, and then began trading and auctioning goods and services over the radio to the listening audience. Within sixty days, the small station was back in the black.

Then the owner bought some cable time. When this also proved successful, investors backed the concept into satellite link, then went national. The stock went up; it grew bigger than Xerox. The company sales now exceed $1 billion, and it all started with 1,400 can openers in trade.

6. *Finance rapid growth without cash*. You don't necessarily have to wait years to amass enough capital to go into business. If you're innovative, you can get started with virtually nothing, and the capital will come to you. Here's what I mean:

Carnival Cruise started out as a Florida-based cruise line. It now has the largest cruise line in the world. But it started with only one ship and no real capital. It was totally uncapitalized. In the beginning, the lone ship the company had wasn't even painted on one side. (I know this because I'm friends with Carnival's marketing and advertising guy.) The company had to park it on the painted side so people wouldn't know the other side was unpainted.

So what Carnival did was trade otherwise-empty cabins for radio, television, and newspaper advertising in 100 cities over a ten-year period. The cost of an empty cabin once the ship sails is minimal, plus the passengers would spend considerable cash in the bar, casino, and gift shop. When the advertiser or other recipients booked the cruise, Carnival would charge them a processing fee of about $90. That $90 paid for all the food plus the incremental cost of towels, toilet paper, and electricity. So Carnival was out nothing, and it got the advertising it needed.

The payoff for Carnival was pretty substantial: The company used this technique to become the largest cruise line in the world, continuously advertising in 100 cities for more than ten years without spending a penny of hard cash. A conservative estimate of the amount of sales generated numbers in the hundreds of millions of dollars. The owner became a billionaire and was on the top of the Forbes Richest Men list—all with this one bartering strategy.

7. Recycle dollars right back into your own pocket. Barter certificates can be used as a type of currency that circulates only within your business. What you pay out comes right back in:

Remember our discussion of the New Orleans hotel? It extended the barter scrip approach beyond that one $125,000 deal. Now it issues its own barter certificates to the tune of $7 million a year. The certificates over the years have become extremely popular. The hotel is able to trade for advertising on nearly any radio or TV station in the country because it's so desirable. It saves an estimated $10 million a year in cash through this process because it gets incremental business and, in any case, honors the certificates only when they're unsold. In short, this way of doing business costs the hotel almost nothing.

Here's another example:

The City of Palm Springs orders advertising for its tourist bureau. In order for the media—the radio stations and the TV stations around the country—to be paid for the advertising they run, the tourist bureau requires that the media travel to Palm Springs and spend the vouchers in the city itself. In other words, the money gets recycled. Let's say the tourist bureau execs spend $100,000 on TV in New York. They don't pay it with cash. Instead, they pay it in vouchers good for any merchant of the tourist bureau in Palm Springs; but it's got to be repaid there, so it all comes back.

One other thing I recommend that businesses do is to leverage stockholder benefits. Many companies issue employee or stockholder benefits, like bonuses, vacations, and so on, in barter. They do it all in barter, and it costs them almost nothing. And it's not just about accumulating perks to pass out to employees. It's about creating revenue that flows direct to the bottom line.

This strategy isn't just for companies working with limited capital. Here are a few of the companies that trade: During the oil shock of the 1970s, Chrysler, stuck with big gas-guzzlers that suddenly no one wanted, traded 900 Imperials in six weeks for radio and TV advertising that helped the company stay alive. Yamaha traded 16,000 guitars for advertising. Mazda traded 350 cars for advertising credits. These companies, too, have successfully made use of bartering: Best Western, Sheraton, Outrigger, the former Beverly Wilshire Hotel, Carnival Cruise, Aero Mexico, KLM, Continental, RCA, Citizen's Watch, Turner Broadcasting System, NBC, Budget Rent-a-Car, Avis, Hawaiian Tropic, Conrad Cruise, Mexicana Airlines, Air France, Curtis Publishing, TWA, Samsung, Carl's Junior restaurants, Levitz Furniture, and Coty Perfume.

All of these companies have traded in the past. I project many more will barter in this crisis economy. One of those should probably be yours.

STRIKING THE RIGHT BALANCE BETWEEN
PAYING TOO MUCH AND PAYING TOO LITTLE

When your business is struggling, it's often possible to narrow down the problem to either paying too much or paying too little. When you're paying too much, it's usually because you have too much fixed overhead that's not earning its keep, which in turn is a result of not measuring and imposing performance expectations on your ROI or not knowing how to maximize performance as revenue streams. When you're paying too little, your employees probably aren't doing their best work.

Here's how you can solve both issues. On the profit-center side, you could use the information you learned in Chapter 4 to change the way your employees are compensated, so that their success is tied more directly to the success (and profitability) of your business. That is, if the business improves, so does their compensation; if profits drop, so does some portion of their compensation.

It basically works like this: Instead of paying a salesman $3,000 per month, you could pay him $2,000 plus a variable, such as a percentage of his total sales or a bonus for each client service call over the daily quota. Of course, your offer has to be fair as well as empathetic to the needs of the salesman; otherwise you won't produce the positive motivation you're after but, rather, will stimulate fear and uncertainty and paralysis, which always negatively impact performance. So make sure that your offer provides a positive incentive and is structured in a way that reflects your support.

With an incentive package, all of a sudden your expense drops. Yet the more you pay, the more you're selling, which in turn means more profits pulled in. Bottom line: Don't just pay for salaries; pay for *results*.

Some specific examples come to mind: Gem dealers give rare gems to top salespeople for their spouses or for themselves; car dealers offer the use of a luxury car like a Mercedes 550SL for the top salesperson of the quarter; and airlines offer employees the benefit of free or reduced travel. These prizes/incentives are appealing to the recipients, who gravitated toward these industries because they liked gemstones, fine cars, or travel to begin with.

To solve the problem of overhead, you can employ the concept of joint venturing and power partnering, which we touched on in Chapter 3 and will explore further in Chapter 10. Remember the podiatrist who rented out space in a sleep clinic and the businessman who went to Indonesia and Malaysia to team up with motorcycle manufacturers? These examples are only a small sampling of the numerous other ways to turn costs from expenses into sales.

By forming strategic alliances—a strategy I like to refer to as "Partner or Perish"—you're putting a twist on the old-fashioned concept of partnering by dramatically expanding and enhancing your business potential. This isn't just a trend. It's a whole new way of doing business, and it's here to stay. To give you an idea of the popularity of strategic alliances, here are a couple of facts:

- More than 20 percent of all the revenue generated from the top 2,000 U.S. and European companies now comes from alliances.

- The number of alliances is growing by 20 percent a year, with an estimated 10,000 new big-business alliances being reported in a single year alone.

We see examples of strategic alliances every day: Think of the bank located within your grocery store, the fast-food restaurants inside retailers such as Home Depot, the Pringles ads encouraging us to wash down their chips with an icy-cold Coke. In each of these cases, both parties are reaping enormous benefits from increased exposure to decreased advertising costs.

The best thing about such alliances is that you can capitalize on them with *no money down*, and with no risk, either—if you do it properly. There's no better way to keep costs from eating up your profits than to simply eliminate the need for initial investments. Let me show you what I mean.

A chiropractor came to one of my programs, really absorbed everything I was offering, and left with the drive and confidence to act on the knowledge he had gained. His home was situated near a big national forest, and every year the rangers at that national forest had to pay people to haul away the pine needles that fell from the trees. The chiropractor learned that if you turn pine needles into mulch, it makes just about the best fertilizer imaginable. Luckily for him, he was the first in the area to make that connection—or, more important, the first to *do* something about it.

He found a trucking firm that passed the national forest on its delivery route. So, he offered the truckers a deal whereby they would pick up the pine needles and deliver them to him for *no up-front fee*, but for a percentage of revenue he would eventually earn. He also found a big used-car lot that was unoccupied and made a deal with the owner, who let him access the space, again, for *no up-front fee*—just a promise of a share in the profits.

Then the chiropractor went to the national forest service and underbid what any of the other hauling companies were asking to take the pine needles away. In fact, he underbid by 50 percent, got the deal, had the trucking company haul the pine needles and the car lot store the pine needles, turned them into mulch—and made $300,000 in the first year from the ingenious joint-venture triumvirate he engineered. And he did all of this without making a risky initial investment in his partners. *That's* the beauty of partnership in action.

HARNESS THE POWER OF PACKAGING
TO INCREASE YOUR PROFITS

There's another strategy I recommend for ensuring that costs don't eat up your profits: the power of packaging. I never sell just a commodity. Rather, I always try to add elements, whether tangible or intangible, to make the product proprietary— incomparable to anything else out there. By packaging a product as proprietary, a business increases its perceived value, maximizing the strategy of preeminence (discussed in Chapter 2).

Most businesses are stuck in "parity pricing," meaning that they have to charge what their competitors are charging— no more, no less—or they won't get the business. But if everyone's pricing is the same, a business owner's success can come only from cutting the price. Unless you have such a presence in the market that you are by far the dominant player, you can't squash everybody around you. And you can't compete on price forever because somebody else will eventually do what you're doing better, faster, or cheaper.

So how can you unstick your business from the parity-pricing predicament? One way is to change the game you're playing by making your offer so different from everyone else's that clients want to buy *only from you*. Here's an example.

Let's say that everyone is selling a computer for $1,995, with a profit of $200. You're moving very few units because everyone is selling at the same price. If you could take $50 of the $200 of profit and use it to buy accessories—software, music downloads, optic mouses, and so on in bulk, at modest distributor pricing (but which the consumer values as substantial)— you can package these high-perceived-value items with the computer as "no-cost" bonus items.

Now you've changed the game. You're no longer selling a commodity. Instead, you're selling *a proprietary package*—full of valuable additions that no one else has thought of. Anyone in their right mind would buy from you over the competition, all other factors being equal. Then you get all the profits from future repeat purchases, too.

EXPAND (OR CONTRACT) YOUR TIME HORIZONS TO STABILIZE AND IMPROVE YOUR CASH FLOW

Foresight can be crucial in planning your company's future. But running a business with an operating horizon set too far in the future is like planning to kayak around the globe in a week. Sometimes you have to take small steps first.

When I used to do turnarounds with corporations, I made sure to look at the rate of cash growth. I asked the CEOs, "At what point does this business reach a critical point of no return?" Every decision and every activity had to have a return on investment with a foreseeable horizon. After all, it didn't matter if something was a great investment if the company was going to survive only six months, whereas the result of the investment wouldn't show for eighteen months! Here's an example of how this problem typically surfaces.

I once helped a company that was in the middle of a software installation that wouldn't be completed for twelve months and wouldn't show a return on investment for thirty-six months. Typically, getting an ROI in twelve to eighteen months is considered a very good outcome. This company, however, had only six months' worth of cash. By the time it started realizing the benefits of that investment, it would be out of business.

I determined the point at which the company would reach a critically low level of cash and then moved back the ROI horizon by 20 to 40 percent, so that every decision being made had an almost immediate return. As the company started to succeed and the cash situation improved, I gradually moved the horizon further out, so as to avoid becoming too crisis-management-oriented.

When it comes to unsticking your business from the "in one way, out the other" trap, it's all about controlling your cash flow so that the right amounts are coming in and out each month. This means plugging up the leaks and taking a long hard look at your ROI; it also means investigating bartering arrangements and packaging options. Get creative, and have fun with this. Because only after you've mastered your cash flow can the *real* fun begin.

Working itself can be part of the fun—unless you're stuck doing what isn't working at all. Now, that's a whole other story.

The Bottom Line

- You *must* measure the return on investment of your marketing. If you're not measuring, you're throwing your money in a sinkhole.

- Measure the performance of each sub-element of generating and sustaining your business: identifying your audience, reaching that audience or enticing them to come to you, and closing the audience on transactions that motivate them to return.

- Adjust your measurement horizon in terms of your overall outlook. If your business is declining, you have to change how you operate.

- Measure everything you do in terms of either an investment or a profit center, as opposed to just a cost expense.

- Achieve a greater return on investment through bartering: Save cash on capital expenditures, print your own scrip, remember that your bartering partner might not cash in, convert your bartered items for cash, create a barter profit center, finance rapid growth without cash, and recycle dollars back to yourself.

■ Recognize when you're paying too much—and when you're paying too little.

■ Package your product as proprietary.

■ Though it's tempting to cut back on marketing in tough times, grit your teeth and do the opposite.

☞ **Immediate Action Step** Take a manageable, low-risk step into the world of bartering by asking yourself what you could offer in a barter relationship *right now.* Get on the phone and close your first barter deal.

7

ARE YOU STUCK STILL DOING WHAT'S NOT WORKING?

How many unsolicited newsletter promotions would you say you get with your mail every month? I'd be willing to bet a good number. They come in all shapes and sizes, and they represent industries as far-reaching as real estate, finances, health, and fitness.

Maybe you drop these newsletters straight into your trash can—or your recycling bin, if you're feeling conscientious—on your way back from the mailbox. But did you know that newsletters are a billion-dollar-a-year business? They also provide one of the most fabulous case studies in businesses that keep doing the same ol' same ol'—long after it's stopped working.

For years and years, businesses sent out conventional sales letters. They stuck them in standard white #10 envelopes with screaming teasers and mailed them out by the thousands. Eventually, they stopped working. But instead of changing their strategy, businesses sent more and more of them.

Then, a few years ago, a man named Lee Euler got the idea to turn the traditional sales letter into a small book. He created a "bookalog"—a little one-hundred-page pocket-book that's actually a sales promotion—and he owned the market. Then everyone started doing bookalogs and they stopped working.

But instead of changing their strategy, businesses sent more and more of them.

A few years after that, a man by the name of Jim Rutz, followed by a marketing master named Gary Bencivenga, got the idea to turn the bookalog into a magalog, a hybrid of magazine and newsletter. The magalog looked liked a magazine with stories, color photos, and articles to pique clients' interest, but underneath all the gloss, it packaged the same message as an old-school sales letter. The difference? It was a whole lot more effective. Magalogs penetrated the market with greater curiosity, interest, and credibility.

This was the evolution of the newsletter. But what's most remarkable about the story, in my opinion, is the fact that, when the old way of doing things stopped working, the vast majority of businesses didn't change their tactics. They just tried to do *more of the same thing*, only more aggressively. They stuck more screaming bullets on the outside of their newsletters, they added more people to their mailing lists, they put more pages in their mailings to try to overwhelm their prospects—all instead of shifting the mechanism to cause more impact.

As we've seen throughout this book, too many executives and entrepreneurs "follow the herd." Even when they're stuck, they don't think there's anything different to do. Most business-people tend to run their companies from the same revenue-generating stance as everyone else in their industry. That simply won't work. If you're doing what everybody else is doing, you aren't differentiating yourself from the competition.

This chapter deals with how to escape "status quo thinking." We'll look at what's working, and at what's not working as well as it could. We'll focus on the importance of examining your processes and the benefits of measuring and testing to achieve higher and better performance. When we're through, you'll be able to spend your time working on the things that are actually going to work for you.

OUT WITH THE OLD, IN WITH THE NEW

If you use the same methods everyone else in your industry uses, you'll be lucky if you surpass anyone. You might even do worse. Everyone is buying and selling, marketing, attending trade shows, and making cold calls the same way—saying the same things, making the same propositions. So how can you expect to do any better when you're doing the same?

To start thinking creatively, you have to get clear on your current practices so that you can expand on what's working and move beyond what isn't. Think about the following questions. They may seem simple, but you'd be surprised how many businesspeople don't consider them when they think about a marketing strategy.

Ten Questions to Ask Yourself to Make Sure You Know What's Working in Your Business— and What Isn't

1. What business are you currently in?

2. What's the market you currently address/serve?

3. How are you reaching that market?

4. How many additional practical ways can you expand, contact, or access that market?

5. What product(s) and/or service(s) can you sell?

6. What additional products/services can you add/offer?

7. How many can you create?

8. Where would you turn to find outside out-sourced producers?

9. Who else has access to the same or related prospective buyers as you?

10. What is the marginal net worth/lifetime value of the initial product or service you sell? (If you're not sure, consult Chapters 9 and 10, where we'll discuss these concepts in detail.) Of the next transaction? Of your total years of revenue?

———————

Let's take a quick inventory. Grab a pen and write out all of your assets and resources. Then, note the skills and abilities at your disposal (your own and those of your team members). List your other assets, too, such as your sales force and your strategic relationships. End by listing your available resources, such as equipment, space, and underutilized skilled labor.

Okay. Now you know your starting point. How do you take it further? Most people's knowledge consists only of what they've learned through observation or training. If you spend the majority of your career in one industry, you're limited to the machinations of that one industry, because you've never been exposed to anything else. It's a conundrum: On the one hand, you're extremely knowledgeable in your industry; on the other, you're extremely knowledgeable *only* in your industry. You may know the best practices for marketing in *toy* manufacturing, but if the marketing practices of *shoe* manufacturing are even better, how would you know?

I've had the good fortune of traveling around the world more than forty times, consulting with industries in nearly as many countries. More important, I've traveled the business world, where I've been involved with 465 different industries— not companies but *different industries*.

Such exposure has allowed me to see myriad ways of thinking and transacting business. I've analyzed almost every method out there, and certain ones always seem to float to the top.

Let's start with a little something I like to call "Funnel Versus Tunnel Vision."

DEVELOP FUNNEL VISION INSTEAD OF TUNNEL VISION— AND MOVE FAR BEYOND BEST PRACTICES

An approach in one industry that is as common as dirt can have a positive effect when introduced in another industry. But you can begin trying new approaches only by first acknowledging that what you're currently doing is highly unlikely to be anywhere close to the most effective, and therefore the most profitable, method available. You need to make a point of exposing yourself to other industries as well as to other strategic ways of thinking, acting, and transacting business so that you can gather new concepts that you can adapt for your own use.

Anyone who's reading this book already has the first ingredient necessary for success in this investigative process: curiosity. Use your innate curiosity to become what I like to call an "investigative marketer" or a "cross-industry marketing detective." Start looking at the processes other industries use to generate and sustain business. Then analyze those processes and break them down into components.

One of the easiest methods of investigative marketing is to ask your clients about their own businesses. If they're reluctant to share, offer to provide the same information about your business in return. Some of the questions you can start with are as follows.

Ask Other Companies How They Do Business— and Learn from Them!

- How does your business sell and market?

- What business strategy, model, and revenue approach do you use?

- What/who do you target demographically?

- What selling system and mechanism do you use (e.g., mailings, cold calls)?

- What processes are part of that mechanism?

- Are any of those processes an industry norm?

- What have you tried in the past versus recently?

Once you've asked these questions, you'll receive answers that will spur a whole new set of questions. Try to get some metrics while you're at it. Then ask your friends and business associates to do the same with their clients or prospects, and compare notes. You'll all benefit from this exercise.

Alternatively, you can try a more homespun method of investigative marketing. On the way home (only if you take the train—don't do this while driving!) or while you're eating lunch, scan the 700 or so different industries in the Yellow Pages and pick out one that looks the most interesting. Then call up a business within that industry, introduce yourself, and ask to pick the executives' brains. Offer to answer the same questions for them. Exchange information and record what you've learned. Or simply walk into a business and try to get sold. Examine the tactics used on you. Suppress the urge to hang up on the next telemarketer and instead listen to his spiel, then dissect how he's trying to sell you. In all these cases, focus on the process, the sequence, the elements. Ask yourself which parts you find most effective and if you can adapt them to your business. Here's an example of how this can work.

I once took a page from the timeshare industry's marketing practices. High-end timeshares, as many of us know, will offer all sorts of perks just to get you on their property—free meals, free hotel nights, and sometimes, for highly qualified prospects, flights to view the property. Timeshares know that if you're willing to accept the offer and they do a good presentation, then they've got a good chance of converting you from prospect to buyer.

I had a client in Pittsburgh who won Ernst & Young's Entrepreneur of the Year award in his category and who sells technology to the chiropractic field. Using the timeshare method of wooing prospects, we invited qualified prospects to Pittsburgh for a weekend at our expense. We put them up, fed them, and paid for their flights. All they had to do was meet with doctors who already owned the equipment and allow us to make a presentation, at which point they could decide if they thought the product was for them or not. The plan was far more successful than just cold calling or sending a DVD: My client's business *more than tripled* by the end of the year.

BUCK THE TREND

A common practice in sales, it seems, is to hire salespeople on commission, put them in charge of a territory, and turn 'em loose. But the mere fact that this is the *common* way of doing things doesn't mean it's the *best* way. Here's why.

A company that sold Yellow Pages had always hired salespeople on commission and then simply sent out its new reps to start selling. But the company was experiencing incredibly high turnover and hiring costs. The sales department spent an inordinate amount of time seeking out job candidates, hiring, and training, only to see many of the salespeople walk away from the job after only a few months. What's more, the company was entrusting a potentially lucrative segment of the marketplace to salespeople who weren't fully mining it.

I came aboard to help their salespeople become more profitably and productively mobilized each and every working day. We created a lead-generating process in which we made rock-solid appointments before we ever went on to present. This allowed salespeople to spend their quality, concentrated time *not* making cold calls door to door but, rather, talking to prospects who'd already been targeted as having *the highest potential to buy*. Sure, this meant bringing in another level of sales support—the team making phone calls to set appointments and the team creating the direct-mail campaigns—but the sales reps could then focus on what they did best: closing a sale. Even that part of the process became easier, because prospects already understood the product's foundational benefit and so required less education.

So instead of employing an old-school sales force, consider upgrading to a highly specialized *assembly line*, matching people with the roles that best complement their strengths; then fine-tune each role for maximum output. Let's say you have an electronics store that just purchased a newspaper advertisement. You've broken down this particular project into four areas—creating the ad, converting calls, converting prospects to buyers, and upselling the buyer. You've identified which of your employees (or outside resources) best fits each task, which has already increased productivity in each of those areas.

Your next step is to maximize the process in each role:

- What can you do to convert more callers into face-to-face prospects? You need to *optimize the initial contact.*

- Now that you have the prospects in front of you, how can you convince more of them to buy? You need to *refine your sales pitch.*

- Lastly, how can you upsell now or convince them to buy again later?

If you continue to ask yourself—and your employees—these questions each step along the way, you'll be able to develop ways of breaking the same old mold that you (and, most likely, the rest of your industry) have been using since the dawn of time. In fact, one of my favorite case histories comes from my own family.

My son was stuck earning $35,000 a year based on sixty hours a week of selling office equipment. Together, we determined the industries that could be predicted to have the highest probability of buying such products. We organized prospects geographically, and he called in advance to set appointments, rather than just showing up on cold calls.

Next, we started testing different methods of contact, by phone and by mail, to establish which pitch worked best to land an appointment. My son then hit each geographic area with his pre-scheduled appointments. His prospects were already prepped, due to his pre-appointment calls and mailings, so his job when he arrived was faster and easier.

By compressing his schedule in this manner, he was able to accelerate and maximize the process of selling. In his first year with this new approach, my son more than doubled his earnings, bringing in $75,000. Oh yes, and he cut his work hours almost in half.

ELIMINATE THE CONSTRAINTS THAT ARE HOLDING YOU BACK

My farsighted friend Rich Schefren, whom you've heard me praise throughout this book, is a big believer in identifying the constraints that keep a business stuck. He has helped countless businesspeople break down barriers and launch their enterprises into a realm of success they never before imagined by showing them that their businesses' success is not limited by abstractions like talent. What Schefren teaches is groundbreaking and will truly revolutionize the way you think about your business: Only the *potential* of your business is determined by your talents, knowledge, commitment, and the amount of time and effort you spend trying to grow it. The actual *success* of your business is determined by your constraints—and whether or not you break free from them.

Most entrepreneurs are slaving away, sacrificing their lives with little to show for it. Why? Because almost all the work they're doing is increasing their potential and not their success. In essence, they're spending their time on false efficiencies. Unless the entrepreneurs can clearly define their current, biggest, and most immediate constraint and what they're doing to eliminate it, the odds are overwhelming that all the work they are doing is merely increasing their potential and little else. The only way to ensure that your actual success will equal your current potential for success is to eliminate the constraints that are holding you back.

The problems you think are holding you back are most likely merely symptoms of underlying hidden constraints in your business. That's why you so frequently feel as though you're spinning your wheels, solving the same problem over and over again. Your most debilitating constraint is often invisible because the pain it causes is felt in multiple places in your business. These constraints explain every frustration and failure you've ever had, why your business isn't growing as quickly as it should, and why less talented entrepreneurs who work far fewer hours than you are getting ahead faster than you are. They also force you to work harder than you need to and to sacrifice important things in life, like spending time with your family and friends and enjoying the fruits of your labor.

You may be only one constraint away from a million-dollar payday. Identifying and eliminating these restraints is like bursting a dam; once they're gone, all the time, energy, and money you've invested in your business will unleash a flood of growth, sales, and profits that will dwarf anything you've experienced before. So, let's now consider six common constraints taken straight from Schefren's playbook—along with what Rich calls the "hammers" you need to break each one of them down.

Constraint #1: The Idea That Mistakes Should Be Avoided at All Costs

Hammer: Screw up every once in a while! If it means you're trying out new solutions and ideas, it's okay. In fact, it's more than okay.

If you're living in constant fear of screwing up, don't be. As long as you move fast but safely, you're taking action, and action creates forward momentum and direction in your business—even if your progress isn't perfect 100 percent of the time.

One reason it doesn't make sense to beat yourself up about a certain course of action is that everything is relative. One advertising guru recommends always using Tacoma font for your ads, and the next guy says Helvetica is the font of the future. One guy advises you to offer a money-back guarantee *and* a redeemable certificate to unsatisfied clients; the other guy says you should offer just the guarantee. How do you know who's right, who's wrong, and, most important, *what will work best for you?*

There's really only one way: Try out each option. Take safe but definitive action to test the new ideas conservatively. Once you've learned your lesson about what works and what doesn't, make your decision to move either toward it or away from it, depending on your results. And if it's a total disaster? Fine; at least now you know, and you won't waste time on it again. Only *action* creates clarity in today's world.

Constraint #2: Flying Blind (Until It's Too Late)

Hammer: Gather intelligence fast and frequently.

Without key metrics that allow you to constantly improve your business, you're basically flying blind. But if you develop a system of fast and frequent intelligence, this constraint is vaporized.

As I've mentioned time and again throughout this book, businesses are seriously constrained when they fail to gather information about how prospects and clients are responding to their products, sales copy, offers, and more. I already told you that 80 percent of new businesses fail within five years, but did you know that the 20 percent that succeed almost always end up taking a route other than the one intended?

For example, almost every large online company today—such as PayPal, Excite, Flickr, and so on—changed the business model it originally started with. Stuck businesses make mistakes about metrics, such as hoping for a higher conversion rate, when they should be striving for more conversions. Successful online businesses, for example, understand their visitors' purpose. The same obviously goes for offline businesses. Good marketing today is about bridging the gap between your prospects' purpose and your business's purpose. The key to doing this is knowing your buyer's buying process.

Constraint #3: Linear Thinking

Hammer: Learn to view your business as a single large system with lots of legs and branches, rather than as a static straight line.

Linear thinking—treating the painful symptoms that your constraints cause but not the constraints themselves—can cost you a mountain of time and money. Viewing your business as one large interconnected system will eliminate the cause of 99 percent of your business problems and challenges. When I see a company that seems to be trying to solve the same old problems over and over again, it's a safe bet that the constraint is linear thinking. Learning to view your business systemically will knock that constraint flat. Think systems, not symptoms.

Here's a simple process to push your thinking out of the linear trap.

- First, identify a problem in your business.

- Then reframe it as a system problem. In other words, move your focus from the "who" to the "what."

- Probe and quantify to get at the root of the problem. You've got to be clear and specific about the problem, and equally clear and specific about the outcome you want.

- Next, finish this sentence: *"The solution is to install a system that will _____."* (Insert the outcome that you want.)

- After that, define the specific system solution and assign someone the task of creating it.

- Finally, implement the solution. And voila! Problem solved.

Constraint #4: An Inefficient Work Style Severely Limits Your Productivity

Hammer: Implement time-savers to quickly maximize your output and profits.

Remember those time-saving strategies we talked about in Chapter 5? They're not just clever ideas—they're ways of *willing* productivity and profit-wise work for you. Put them in place now! You haven't a second to lose.

Here's a challenge: Unplug your computer from the Internet for one twenty-four-hour period. See what it's like without the constant ball-and-chain of e-mail. I guarantee you, you'll be at least 150 percent more productive. And the feeling of freedom will be intoxicating.

Constraint #5: Being Alone and Lost in a Networked World

Hammer: Create a worldwide personal network of quality business players (i.e., a mastermind group, a board of advisors, or a private group of mentors—call it whatever you want to) who will help you solve any problem your business encounters—and fast, because they've already faced and overcome such problems themselves.

Let me be clear here: When I say you must have a strong personal network today, I'm talking about people you can call on *anytime* to help you solve a business problem or seize an emerging opportunity—and to do it faster and better than your competitors. At the very least in today's wired world, you need three types of people in your network:

1. People who either have the *answers* you need or can connect you to the ones who do

2. People who have the *resources* you need

3. People who can perform *specialized tasks* far better than you—or anyone on your staff

We'll cover this topic in much greater detail in Chapter 8.

Constraint #6: Customer Bottlenecks in Your Sales Process

Hammer: Rip the lid off your customer's constraints and develop a continuous forward pressure that advances and maximizes all sales potential.

The same factors that have increased the power of the customer have also made the purchase decision more difficult. In *Paradox of Choice*, Barry Schwartz shares a study that perfectly illustrates this elongation of the buying process. A group of shoppers was offered the opportunity to sample a selection of premium jams. Half were offered six samples, and the other half were offered twenty-four. Whereas 30 percent of the shoppers in the six-sample group went on to buy some jam, only 3 percent (90 percent fewer) of the people in the twenty-four-sample group bought anything! As they say, the key to happiness is having fewer choices.

The good news is that, like everything else in our businesses, the buying process is a system. And as with all systems, its constraints can be quickly eliminated once you surface them. That's crucial when it comes to shortening the length of the buying process among your clients. The increase in buying speed leads to buyer momentum and that reduces buyer's remorse—which in turn leads to lower refund rates.

So what benefits will you get from removing these six constraints? First and foremost, you and your business will attain success much more quickly and with less effort. You'll reclaim your personal life and family life once again, and you'll enjoy it more because you'll have more energy (because you are working less) and fewer worries (because you are earning more). You'll achieve optimal positioning in the market, and you'll do it fast.

MANAGE YOUR SALES FORCE

In my many years of working with businesses in those 465 industries, I've noticed that most salespeople aren't trained in the art of persuading, motivating, and influencing people—and those, of course, are the key elements of consultative selling, which we explored in Chapter 3. We've talked about changing the way your sales force sells. Now let's talk about specific ways to ensure that your sales force runs as well as (or better than) a smoothly oiled machine.

When reinvigorating a sales force, I always start by being pragmatic. I break down the process into two stages:

- Stage 1 is about *maximizing what you're already doing*. Optimization before innovation, remember? I say this not because what you're doing is a best practice or because it's entrenched in your system, but because you might as well make it pay off more than it already is. This way, you can use the increased profit to fund the development and, eventually, the installation of the replacement methods that you then implement in the later part of Stage 2.

- Stage 2 is where you look at the data, which open the door for *innovation*. Zero in on the different subprocesses of sales and identify the best salespeople for each. Who opens the most accounts? Who's better at selling different kinds of products? Who's better at selling one particular product? Who's better at reselling? Who's better at maintaining accounts?

Once you've identified who, identify *why*: Why do those individuals dramatically outperform their peers in that category? If you can recognize those elements of success, you then ask yourself, Can I teach that skill to everybody? If not, am I better off having this individual own that subprocess and perform this function exclusively (or at least primarily for my business)?

Let's say you have six salespeople, and that your analysis showed you that Todd was ten times better than anyone else at opening new accounts but not so great at maintaining. You also found out that Laura was five times better at selling your product to car dealers and that Leah was four times better at maintaining accounts. You're now faced with two choices.

Choice 1 is to teach your salespeople's individual methods to everyone to improve each of those areas by 10 to 20 percent. This would result in an overall sales improvement of perhaps 300 percent.

Your other choice is to have Todd be in charge of opening new accounts, which he then turns over to Leah to maintain. After all, that's more pragmatic than asking Todd to maintain accounts, given that Leah is better at it. But you can't know the answer if you don't ask the question to begin with, which is why analysis of your processes is so vitally important. Let's look at a real-life example.

I recently met with an advertising company that employed 400 salespeople. This company had the same model as all its competitors: It would provide new hires with four weeks of a token salary, and from there, the new hires worked purely on commission. The sales force spent all of its time knocking on doors, pitching services, and getting deals.

On the surface, the approach looked cost effective, especially because it's how things have always been done in that industry. The company was actually enjoying growth, albeit moderate growth, so the top managers didn't believe they had a problem.

However, I saw their approach to sales as completely opportunity-cost *ineffective*. I showed them that they were spending a fortune on advertising and training, with almost nothing to show for it. I told the managers that their company would be better off utilizing high-quality, prospect space ads, direct mail, and seminars to target only the highest-probability future clients and clients. Then, creating set appointments with those clients would ensure that the company's *income-generators* (my term for "salespeople") would spend all of their time in the field, talking to highly valuable prospects who were already predisposed toward buying, instead of wasting most of their time looking for the chance to "pitch" to just anybody.

The result? This approach led to an immediate and dramatic increase in sales by a factor of 5 within the first six months. *That's* geometric growth.

DON'T LET THESE THINGS HAPPEN TO YOU

I see so many business owners continuing to repeat the same blunders time and again. What's worse is that many of them *know* they're making mistakes, but they continue to do so for lack of a better idea. We've talked about some of the ways businesses get stuck with strategies and practices that just aren't working. Now I want to share the other most common mistakes I see repeated by businesses across industries.

Failing to Follow Through and Follow Up

I can't tell you how often I see businesses failing to follow through. Following through is imperative in all areas of business, but nowhere more so than in sales. Following through—and its counterpart, following up—reactivates clients, reminding them that you exist and keeping your product in their heads so that they repurchase or even refer you to others. A simple call can cause a chain reaction of benefits.

Never Trying Something New

Another blunder is never trying on new words, phrases, or proposition positionings for size. There's always a different way to get your point across. I once had a very large furniture company try thirty-three different ways of greeting people at the front door. We discovered that one approach alone produced triple the number of sales. All we had to do was come up with a few new words—a very inexpensive investment for a threefold sales increase.

Not Testing and Analyzing Your Approach to Your Business

Then there's testing and analysis, which we looked at in Chapter 5. I can't emphasize enough how important this is. I once worked with one of the largest multivariable testing organizations in the world, and I'm not exaggerating when I say that this company tested billions of dollars' worth of variables—everything from changes in manufacturing through output, to what happens if you move different products around in retail stores. Changing signage, coming up with different combinations of integrated communications, modifying various elements in the sales contact and follow-up processes—you name it, this company has tested it. And the piece of information I found most intriguing? Sometimes one change will cause marginal movement, and a second change will do likewise—but the two together could produce a seismic shift up to thirty times greater.

All of these are examples of *optimization*—using what you've got to work with, and making it work differently. Innovation, as earlier defined, is the decision to try something entirely new. If you're still stuck doing what's not working, chances are you're missing the buck when it comes to innovation. Why is this problem so prevalent?

Being Afraid to Try Something New

Fear of the unknown often holds the blame. Sure, uncertainty can be scary. The key to eliminating fear is to give yourself permission to fail, because you're probably going to do so a few times—maybe even more than a few. Remember Constraint

#1? Not every action is going to be successful. But if you don't try something new, you'll *never* achieve success.

As an analogy, think of someone you know who's been gaining weight and putting off dieting. He spends all day on the couch eating Cheetos and watching *SportsCenter*. If he doesn't change his ways, he'll just continue increasing his waistline and compounding the misery in his life.

Or, he could review his options. He could realize that he needs to burn more calories and consume less food. He could eat more nutritious food—not necessarily fewer calories, but *different* calories. Each of those options holds the potential to get to a better place, but he'll never get there if he doesn't first ask the right questions and then opt for the easiest, most non-threatening first step.

An innovation is nothing more than the recombination of old elements and facts that you already knew. Your capacity to bring old elements into new combinations depends largely on your ability to see relationships. To some, each fact is a separate bit of information, while to others it's a link in the chain of knowledge. Indeed, from my own perspective, each fact is an illustration of a general law.

FIVE EASY STEPS TO CHANGE THE WAY YOU DO BUSINESS

Once you have identified a specific question, problem, or challenge for your business (or your life) that you want to address, you can consult this list of five steps for creating the new relationships between elements that will lead to a solution:

1. Gather raw material—specific information about your business and industry as well as general information that you observe about the world, human beings, the way things work, and so on. Don't look

to heaven for inspiration. Work systematically. Write down whatever strikes you as useful or relevant, or just plain interesting. Use 3-by-5 cards for easy access.

2. Allow things to gestate. This step happens in your head, but as creative bursts about specific building blocks come forth, write them down. Use those 3-by-5 cards again.

3. Forget about it all for a while. Put the challenge out of your mind. Turn it over to your subconscious mind.

4. Even though you're not actively thinking about new ideas, write them down as they occur to you. A surprisingly good idea will miraculously appear, seemingly out of nowhere, when you are least expecting it. Write it down immediately; capture it on paper forever.

5. Finally, in the cold, gray sobriety of morning, examine it for review and revising. A good idea will expand and evolve—so be willing to make adjustments, ask for input, and keep refining, improving, and perfecting it.

Unfortunately many company owners, when their businesses get stuck, don't think there's anything different to do. They're blinded by their failure and often find themselves in a state of paralysis: They just can't see a way out.

This doesn't have to describe you any longer. Don't be like the thousands of business owners who continue to mail out tired, clichéd newsletters to people who don't read them. Instead, think ahead to the bookalog stage, or start a revolution with magalog-level success. In short, find a more powerful, more credible, more meaningful way to impact the market.

And if the market repays you by relegating you to the margins? Well, I've got the solution for that, too.

The Bottom Line

- If you're doing what everyone else is doing, you aren't differentiating yourself from the competition—and you're probably stuck.

- Ask yourself the ten basic questions I've outlined to make sure you know what is and isn't working in your business strategy.

- Think outside the industry box. Look at the processes other industries use to generate business, then break them down into components. Can you adapt them to your business?

- Turn your sales force into a highly specialized assembly line. Be pragmatic; optimize strengths and eliminate weaknesses.

- Identify the constraints in your business that are holding you back—and take a hammer to them.

- Reinvigorate your sales force through optimization and innovation.

- Don't get stuck failing to follow through and follow up, failing to try something new, failing to analyze and test your approach, or being afraid of change.

■ When you need to get creative, take these five easy steps: Gather raw material, allow things to gestate, forget about it for awhile, write down every new idea, and finally, review and revise.

☞ **Immediate Action Step** Call a client right now and have a conversation about his or her marketing strategy. Once you have even one such conversation, you will quickly develop an appetite for more!

8

ARE YOU STUCK BEING MARGINALIZED BY THE MARKETPLACE?

The starting point for success is your vision of yourself. If you believe you're a commodity, then you're a self-fulfilling prophecy. And worse yet, if you behave just like everyone else, then you've already accepted your business's death sentence: allowing it to be marginalized by the marketplace.

A few years ago, I had client named Greg who owned a financial service business that sold guaranteed return annuities. Unfortunately for Greg, he wasn't the only one selling guaranteed return annuities. He was knocking on doors and running ads in the *Wall Street Journal*, but he had done nothing to distinguish himself from his competitors. As a result, his business was marginalized; his prospects saw no difference between his services and all the comparable offerings on the market.

It didn't look good for the future of Greg's business. That is, until the day he got the wild idea of finding someone—me—to endorse him as the "guaranteed return annuity provider" for twenty different newsletters. (In other words, invest your money with him, and you'll make more—guaranteed.)

It was a brilliant way of setting himself and his business apart. Within the first six months of having my endorsement, Greg did $60 million exclusively. And because he had direct access to cream-of-the-crop investors from the newsletters, he rapidly became the only game in town. Greg went from struggling and selling a few million dollars to selling $60 million—and all by simply setting himself apart from his competition.

In this chapter, we'll talk about how to avoid the pitfalls of *marginalization* and *commoditization*—the twin demons that keep most businesses from attaining geometric growth. The world wants to marginalize and commoditize businesses; I want to show you how to strike back.

It's all about knowing how to distinguish yourself, your business, and your product/service in ways nobody else does. Do that, and you'll have succeeded in making yourself stand out. Soon you'll vanish from the world of commoditized companies without a trace.

The secret is yet another set of three P's: Be preeminent, be preemptive, and be proprietary.

BE PREEMINENT IN YOUR FIELD

Preeminence is a matter of "surpassing all others." You should be striving for greatness—not greatness in yourself, but in your impact and contribution to the marketplace. But that's not possible if you don't start with a vision of the superior value and difference that you bring to the transaction. (You must clearly recognize what your marketplace most specifically serves, too.) Unless you already have an established brand with an unprecedented value of its own, you don't have anything different physically. But you *can* have something profoundly different in terms of the way you integrate and render it.

The difference starts with an intentional factor that precedes the transaction itself: your mindset and attitude. From there, it's only a matter of time before the people you want to impact most—namely, your most coveted prospects—will do business with you.

Why? Because you care more, do more, serve better, provide a better outcome. Bottom line? You're a better investment than anyone else out there.

With that in mind, why wait for money to change hands to make a difference? When you adopt this mindset, your prospects will soon become your clients, all because your way of relating to them is totally different from that of your competitors.

And that's when you'll receive your well-earned compensation. The sooner you start improving your clients' lives, the sooner they'll recognize the different value you bring compared to your generic competitors. So don't waste any time!

Simply adopting a preeminent mindset overrides all else. You then evolve that mindset into an understanding that when you interact, either directly or indirectly, your goal is to make your prospects look toward that golden tomorrow from the very start, and to make them understand that you're the only one who can deliver it to them.

In your mind, you no longer even have competitors. As former NFL quarterback Steve Young put it, "The principle is competing against yourself. It's about self-improvement, about being better than you were the day before." You're now competing against yourself to see how much more value you can bring to the transaction—even before it's transacted.

Your next step is to see how much additional certainty and clarity you can bring to your clients' lives in each and every contact, all the while maintaining a clear vision of how much better off your clients will be—not just because of your product or service alone but also because of all the support that comes with it. You're not thinking this out of arrogance; you're thinking it because you know how much more committed you are to achieving a greater outcome for them. You have to honestly want to provide your client with the best future possible through your problem-solving.

Once you've accomplished that step, it's time to move up to that rarefied level of ethos, integrity, and service that most businesspeople don't even realize is possible: becoming your clients' most trusted advisor. You provide them with a keen assessment of what you would do if you were in their shoes, knowing what you know. You balance that confidence with humility, which means that when approaching unknown territory, you take the time to get the lay of the land and educate yourself before proceeding. You admit when you lack knowledge on a subject, then you seek out the answers to inform both yourself and the client. Clients love dealing with real people who care deeply about their hopes, dreams, fears, and desires.

You have to feel deep down in your heart that, in your niche, you are the absolute best outcome for the transaction your prospect is being asked to make. Because if you're not dealing in full integrity, you can't in good conscience justify proceeding with the transaction.

Developing this confidence may sound intimidating, but confidence is simply a function of certainty in behalf of your client's best interests. Consider the three options your clients have aside from you, which I discussed in Chapter 5:

- They can buy from you instead of buying from your competition.

- They can buy from you instead of choosing an alternative form of solving their problem or fulfilling their opportunity.

- They can buy from you instead of doing absolutely nothing.

Your job is to evaluate the pros and the cons of each and figure out how you can excel beyond any of those options so that you can justify your confidence.

In reaching for preeminence—in effect, striving to "surpass all others"—you're seeking to make the most money and squash your competitors. But while that is the final goal, you must first surpass the others in providing *added value* and *empathic connection*. These sources of comfort are ultimately what will compel people to pay a premium for your product instead of your competitor's. You can't ask for a premium if you're actually a subpar provider or have nothing unique or valuable to offer.

With the thought of "surpassing all others" playing in your mind, you can approach the transaction from the standpoint of your clients. Most of your competitors do not know how their clients live their lives. And most do not understand transactions from their clients' perspective. That's why *you* start there. You then see how many different ways you can add dimension to value—value that is appreciated not by you but by *them*.

Sometimes it's simply a matter of making the final connection for your client. For example, you might say, "We've perfected the art of production, which has led to less variation." "So what?" says the client. So, you make that final connection for them. You can answer confidently, "My perfectly produced product with less variation performs ten times longer—with one-tenth the failure rate." Knowing that, the client can see your product's advantage over the others. You just have to explain it from his perspective.

As with cars and baseball players, those businesspeople who surpass all others are the ones most coveted. But you can't attain that status if you don't have a systematic, strategic, sustaining plan to get there and stay there. Remember: Because preeminence is judged on the basis of achievement or contribution, your plan must be externally focused, meaning that your client's benefits—not your own—are what you're working toward, always. Here's an example from my own career.

When I started on my career path, I had no money or clients. I did, however, have significant experience and knowledge gained from starting my own business and working for other companies, as well as the innate ability to motivate people to take action. That ability was a value-added quality that I believed could translate into untold profits for my clients—while also promising less effort, stress, and risk than they were already facing.

So, from the very beginning I asked a premium price for my services, because I believed I could offer something to my clients that my competitors in marketing consulting could not: *action.* It wasn't arrogance that led me to this conclusion but, rather, the heartfelt belief that I would be helping people in a way and at a level of impact that no one else was capable of. I felt that, left to their own devices, most businesspeople might learn the concepts I was trying to teach them, but never use them due to lack of motivation. My knowledge wasn't the distinguishing factor—*everyone* had basic knowledge, more or less. What I brought was the extra catalytic element: the ability to make things happen very profitably for the people I helped.

I started my rates at $2,000 per hour for consulting and $5,000 for seminars, at a time when the average marketing consultant charged $100 per hour and the average seminar cost $495. Over the years, my hourly rate has risen to $5,000 and my seminars are now in the $15,000–$25,000 range, which is still premium.

My point is not to brag. Instead, I want to share how I started out above the rest because of my unique and intangible value.

Here's some news that may shock and surprise you: Every businessperson *wants to feel special, unique, and valuable.*

Here's some more shocking news: *That's okay.*

Wanting to feel unique and valuable is natural and human, whether you're in business or not. Yet most people don't know how to escape their current situation and fast-track their way to greatness. Let me share another example of the power of the strategy of preeminence—and how I used it to teach an obscure postal clerk with a meager government paycheck to turn himself into the number-one maven in his market, with $500 million in sales—that's a half-*billion* dollars.

A few years back, Jim Cook was a postal clerk, sorting mail in a small Minnesota town. But like you—like any of us—he had big dreams. Jim was fed up with his dead-end job and struggling every month to make ends meet. He wanted something more, something better, for himself and for his family. He dreamed about being his own boss, starting a wildly successful company, building a family fortune, and never having to worry about money again. So one day, Jim summoned the courage to walk into his supervisor's office and quit.

It was the 1970s, a time when gold and silver prices were soaring and rare gold and silver coins were skyrocketing in value. So Jim founded a small rare-coin dealership, hung out his shingle, and waited for the money to begin rolling in.

But it didn't.

Jim was at a loss. He did the best thing he could think of—he decided to begin doing all the same things he saw his larger, more successful competitors doing. He rented mailing lists and mailed thousands of postcards offering his product. He bought expensive ads in financial publications. He even paid big bucks to have an exhibit booth at investment conference and trade shows. But with all that expense and risk—not to mention years of grueling work—Jim's tiny company was still bringing in only about $300,000 a year.

In many respects, Jim was facing the same challenges many businesspeople are dealing with today. He had thousands of competitors, most of whom dwarfed his small company, and some had massive advertising budgets and sold hundreds of times more coins than he did. And to top it off, Jim felt he wasn't born with a natural gift for marketing. Nor did he have an encyclopedic knowledge of his industry. He wasn't better looking or more charismatic or more outgoing or a better public speaker than the folks running the show for his larger competitors. And he certainly didn't have the money to fund a national marketing campaign. Jim was getting marginalized in a big and painful way.

I accepted Jim as a client because I saw three crucial qualities in him: a driving, palpable desire to succeed; a fierce desire to contribute far more to his clients; and a willingness to try something new—something more innovative than anyone else in his industry was doing—to light the fuse on explosive sales growth.

My vision for Jim was a simple one—to lift him head and shoulders above his thousands of competitors. Not by spending what little money he had on direct mail or print ads or duplicating the hyperbolic and high-pressure sales tactics his largest competitors used—but by establishing Jim as America's leading precious-metals authority, the *trusted voice* on rare and precious-metals investing.

Instead of writing ads and spending a fortune on media, we went to work creating content-rich, educational articles and special reports to help investors profit. And instead of selling that content, we gave it all away *free* to a handful of influential people who published large-circulation investment newsletters. Within weeks, those publishers began running Jim's articles in their newsletters and offering Jim's special reports to their readers. And soon, the local and then national media began calling Jim to get his views on the explosion in precious metals and coin prices.

Almost before you could say "Rare Coin Maven," millions of people knew who Jim was: the voice of authority in his market. And Jim began fielding thousands of calls and visits from people who wanted to buy rare coins and bullion from him. Suddenly, Jim's tiny $300,000-a-year coin business exploded. And Jim Cook and his company, Investment Rarities, were raking in $500 million a year in gross sales—a half-billion dollars—in just 1½ years. That's a staggering 16,667 percent sales explosion! And he achieved that success not by outworking the competition. Not by outspending them. Not even with red-hot sales copy. But simply by allowing me to establish him as *the preeminent figure* of educational contribution in his industry.

I think this example raises a very interesting question. If Jim did it, *why can't you?* Greg, the financial-services provider

I described at the beginning of this chapter, employed a similar strategy, and it worked wonders for him. Certainly, going from $300,000 to $500 million isn't going to happen for everyone. But there's no reason you can't multiply your sales and magnify your profit picture markedly.

Think about it: Do people want to work with the one who surpasses all others in their knowledge or contribution, or do they want to deal with the average Joe? I think you know the answer to that one:

Be the one who surpasses all others.
Strive for preeminence in all you do.

BE PREEMPTIVE: KNOW WHY YOUR PROSPECTS AND CLIENTS MAY HESITATE TO BUY FROM YOU

Being preemptive means dealing in advance with all the factors that keep a client from moving forward or making a choice. In short, you need to prove how you've overcome numerous obstacles that your competitors haven't even acknowledged. Here's an example.

A friend of mine named Bradley enjoys a successful career training investors in how to make money in real estate. The marketplace is flooded with competitors in his role. However, when prospects ask him how he differs from a well-known competitor in his niche, Bradley replies, "I'm better at what I do for you. My competitor is very good at what she does. But I approach your fate and financial path with a much greater commitment to getting you there quickly, easily, safely, enjoyably, and more predictably than any of my competitors do. I protect your downside better, multiply your upside more, and show you more ethical short-cuts, quick fixes, and fast-track strategies that you can use." By describing himself in this way, Bradley is preempting everyone else.

One of the best preemptive methods is to work candidly with your prospect to compile a pros-and-cons list. Have your prospective client draw up a list with the name of your product or service placed alongside two alternative options that he or she is considering. The rest is easy: Show how you're the optimal choice. After following the steps to preeminence we just considered, you can handle this task with confidence and clarity, because you know you're the best option. Business is a science and, as such, works much like the biomechanics of athletic performance: If something's not working, it's usually due to a functional problem that can be corrected. But you'll never even get a shot at correcting it if you allow your competitors to preempt you.

So, how do you preempt your competition? You can accomplish this by taking the following steps:

1. First, preempt any concern that's holding back your client by acknowledging that concern and overcoming it. Think about Bradley, the real-estate investor I just mentioned. He starts by acknowledging the distinctions between him and his main competitor. Then he explains exactly what he can do that she can't.

2. Second, preempt your client's lack of confidence in the outcome by clearly stating your certainty in the plan and describing what the steps and results will be like and how you will deliver a better desired outcome for your client. In much the same way, Bradley puts an emphasis on the predictability of his approach and describes for his clients his process for protecting their downside.

3. Third, if your client does not perceive the advantages inherent in working with you, preempt this

tendency by helping him establish specific buying criteria, including value-added follow-up or transactional additions such as products or services. This is the clincher, as Bradley has demonstrated. After eliminating risk for his client, he goes on to describe the *benefits* he provides. What he offers is not a simple transaction but a value-added transaction.

Once you've mastered the strategy of preemption, it's time to grasp the third and final P: Be proprietary.

BE PROPRIETARY: *OWN* YOUR MARKETPLACE

If you follow the first two steps in this chapter—be preeminent and be preemptive—you're already well on your way to the third.

If you look up "proprietary" in the dictionary, you'll find it defined as "of or relating to an ownership." With the first two steps accomplished, you have the ownership of the marketplace's top-mind awareness, because you stand out as decisively different. Even though you're public in your actions, others can't compete because they don't understand the elements and thus cannot integrate them.

I mentioned earlier in this chapter that there are two serious threats facing businesses today; being commoditized is one of them. Commoditization means that the products or services you offer are rendered widely available and interchangeable with those provided by another company. In other words, you're no longer special or unique. *And that's no good.*

Shifting from commodity to proprietary is almost a no-brainer—and yet few entrepreneurs understand that. As an example, let's say that everybody is selling the same widget at roughly the same price. You must act quickly to claim ownership of the superior product on the market. One idea is to build value add-ons, such as complementary products and/or services, into the sale for the same basic purchase price—anything that makes you incomparable.

Let's say you're selling a widget that goes for $100, with a full margin of 40 percent. The market climate is so aggressive, though, that most competitors are getting only $22, at best, off each sale. However, *you* have read this book, so you decide to put into action all that you've learned about getting unstuck. Most people would focus on the competition of selling the widget when the real opportunity lies in starting a sustainable relationship that will repeat multiple times per year, making you $2,200 in the long run.

That means that your job is to appeal much more irresistibly to the market to make your product proprietary, a process we explored at the end of Chapter 6. Using what you learned in that chapter, you know that you can take your small margin and use it to purchase an additional product or service that will increase the newly packaged product beyond its $100 market value. Because you're still asking for the same price, however, your offer is seen as being considerably more desirable than anything else out there, and thus proprietary, while your competitor's offer is generic—indistinguishable from that of anyone else in the marketplace.

Believe it or not, the latest research in neuroscience actually works in your favor when it comes to establishing yourself as proprietary. There's a part of the brain called the reticular activating system (RAS). It's believed to be the center of arousal and motivation in all animals and humans. But the RAS has another function—and for business owners, that function is what makes the RAS the most important part of clients' and prospects' brains. Before I explain this crucial function, let me ask: Have you experienced either of the following situations?

- *Situation #1.* You just bought a new car, or became interested in a particular car—and all of a sudden, you start seeing that car all over the place. Obviously they've always been there, but you didn't notice them before. Now you do.

- *Situation #2.* You're at a party, and you're deeply engrossed in a conversation with another person. Of course, lots of other people are talking as well, and you hear a murmur of all these other conversations. You're not really making out what the other people are saying because you're paying attention to the conversation that you're engaged in. But then—your full name is mentioned in one of those peripheral conversations. In an instant, your attention shifts to the person who just mentioned your name.

So, what's going on here? Your brain is continuously taking in millions of details, but because your conscious mind could never handle them all at once, a filter is necessary to keep you sane. That's where the RAS comes in. It's the part of your brain that decides whether you notice or not. It makes the decision in a fraction of a millisecond based on what you already have in your memory. That's why you distinctly hear your name despite the din at a party or notice that new car everywhere you look.

Imagine what you could accomplish if you were able to leverage the RAS as a marketing tool. Wouldn't it be amazing to stake a permanent claim inside the minds of your prospects and your clients? Their RAS would always notice you as important—so your messages would always be read first, your offers would get preferential consideration, your reputation would be defended in every nook and cranny of the Internet and the media world, multiplying your earnings immediately and dramatically.

The RAS isn't the only component of human neuropsychology that can work to your benefit. As Seth Godin recently wrote in a blog post, "Why do some ideas have more currency than others? Because we believe they should. When Chris Anderson or Malcolm Gladwell writes about something, it's a better idea because *they* wrote about it." This phenomenon is called the *placebo effect*. If you establish yourself as proprietary, your clients will get better results, your prospects will have a higher regard for your products and information, and your reputation will actually be extended by your market.

WALK IN YOUR CLIENT'S SHOES

In today's economy, consumers are marginalizing sellers because of the marginalization they're experiencing in their own lives. They're feeling increasingly stressed, unappreciated, and unfulfilled, due to all the pressures they experience on a daily basis, whether financial, work-related, or family-based. Every day, these symptoms manifest themselves in road rage, hypertension, divorce—and the list goes on.

Just the other day, I found myself blowing up at an American Express agent who was assisting me with a credit-card challenge. I'd already had four similar confrontations that day—except that I was on the receiving end of the anger—and I in turn took it out on this hapless agent who had the misfortune of answering my call. Afterward I felt really awful about it, but of course that didn't change the fact that it happened and that similar scenarios occur every second in every corner of the world.

We take out our frustrations on unsuspecting strangers every day, never stopping to acknowledge that these people have hopes and dreams just like we do. We don't stop to think about their problems, whether they're worried about putting their kid through school or just trying to make it home in time for dinner. It doesn't seem to faze us that we could be compounding an already lousy day, or ruining what might be the best day of their life.

All of those factors are real. As a businessperson—and as a human being—you can better the lives of your clients by appreciating who they are and what they do, by letting them know that you're here to assist them and that your product or service will help them with at least one of their conundrums. But you've got to clearly see the connection between who they are and what you're selling. If your product is a word processor, you have to envision your clients as being able to write letters more easily and professionally. If it's insurance, you need to reassure them that they'll be covered should an accident befall them. You see your job in a whole new context. And because you see it with excitement, you transfer that excitement to them, which improves their experience with the transaction. They feel special, because they feel special *to you.*

I learned early on in my career that everybody—present company included—wants to be respected, appreciated, and loved. And the easiest way to be loved is to love in return. As I mentioned earlier, you need to *fall in love with your clients*—as well as with your staff and vendors—and genuinely seek to make their lives better through the work you do for them and the acknowledgement, respect, and appreciation you give them.

How do you make people feel special? By being mindful of their needs. It can be as simple as saying hello when you pass a staff member in the hall, or taking the time to chat with a repeat client about his family. It's sending greetings to clients on their birthdays, or remembering who is earning her MBA at night school and who just retired after forty years with the same firm. I smile at people and engage them even if I don't know them, and especially if others have grown accustomed to overlooking them, as in the case of custodians or doormen.

All of the individuals you interact with each day have their own stories and are important to their own families and jobs. And acknowledging this fact as a part of your everyday thinking is fundamental to improving your client relations. If you honor this principle in your dealings with everyone you meet, it will follow you into your business practices, and your clients will notice.

You might be surprised to find ideas about empathy and human understanding in a book on business. Perhaps you're even a bit shocked to learn that you have to care more about the client than you do about your business. Most clients who come to me with a concern about their business turn the focus internally: How can we cut costs? How can we survive? How can we do better? But the right question to ask is this:

How can I add more value for our clients?

That's where the huge leverage lies.

I find this concept quite liberating, which is why I have so much fun with my work. My sphere of interaction is worlds apart from the thankless, browbeating methods most businesspeople use when they're burdened by a fruitless paradigm. The principles in this chapter are ones that most businesspeople, and most laypeople, don't take the time to work on. And, frankly, it's why they end up being marginalized, stressed, and stuck. That doesn't have to be your future.

Consider yourself off the margins and back on the page. You *are* preeminent, preemptive, and proprietary. You've got the product or service that everyone is dying to have.

Now it's time to turn our attention to making sure *everyone else* knows they're dying to have it, too.

The Bottom Line

■ If you believe you're a commodity, then you'll become a self-fulfilling prophecy.

■ Marginalization and commoditization are the twin demons that are holding your business back from the geometric growth you could attain.

■ Be preeminent in the marketplace: prove that you're a better investment than anyone else out there.

■ You can be your client's most trusted advisor. Operate from a position of integrity and service.

■ Being preeminent means that you surpass all others in *added value* and *empathetic connection*.

■ Being preemptive means that you anticipate the reasons that your clients hesitate to buy from you and assuage those fears.

■ There are three steps to preemption: Preempt the concerns that hold your client back, preempt your client's fears about the outcome, and preempt your client's inability to see the advantage of choosing you.

■ Be proprietary by owning the marketplace. You can't be a commodity if the market is your market.

■ Leverage the neurological concept of the reticular activating system (RAS) as a marketing tool. Make sure your message is the one that's read first, that your offers get preferential consideration, and that your reputation is being defended and upheld.

■ Leverage the *placebo effect*: If your clients expect you to be proprietary, you will be.

■ Fall in love with your clients, your staff, and your vendors.

■ Keep the focus external: How can you add more value for your clients?

☞**Immediate Action Step** List the three to five most common objections your prospects have about you or about what you offer. (Part of President Obama's campaign strategy was to acknowledge that he "doesn't look like any of the presidents on the dollar bills"!) Ask yourself how you can address them in advance every time, and thus get them off the table.

9

ARE YOU STUCK WITH MEDIOCRE MARKETING?

Most entrepreneurs fail to understand that the difference between mediocrity and making millions has more to do with *marketing* than with any other single business factor. Marketing has a geometric capability to propel a business upward. And yet, it's often at the bottom of a business's priority list.

My definition of marketing is simple—it's all about educating the marketplace that your business can solve problems, fill voids, or achieve opportunities and goals the way no other business can. These are problems, voids, opportunities, and goals that consumers and business prospects might not have been able to verbalize before, making it all the more important that you *can*. A business that can clearly and powerfully convey its ability to address these concerns for the prospect will experience outstanding growth—certainly in good times, but in bad times as well.

Marketing is the bedrock of virtually every enduring business, which makes being a superior marketer crucial to your business' success. The good news is that great marketers are made, not born. Marketing efficiently is actually quite simple, despite all the complexity that many authors and so-called experts have brought to the table. Because 99.9 percent of a business's competitors couldn't market their way out of a paper bag, a business that can market even *slightly* more effectively will be the one-eyed man in the land of the blind. If you really take marketing's power seriously, you can own your marketplace.

In this chapter, I'll show you how to achieve true 20/20 marketing vision. You'll see your business grow exponentially as a result.

MARKETING'S ROLE IN YOUR BUSINESS

Although I see myself as a business-growth strategist, I've been categorized as a "marketing guru" or "marketing wizard" for much of my professional career, mainly because I honor marketing's Midas-like role with more understanding than most people. I know without a doubt that for small- to medium-sized businesses, the difference between mediocrity and prosperity can be found mainly in marketing, with strategizing a close second.

Knowing that, I'm shocked to find that the vast majority of businesspeople don't market. At all. They merely hope and dream. The few who do some form of marketing do so intermittently and erratically, with very little strategy driving their actions, activities, or decisions. Marketing can be the most highly leveraged investment a business can ever make, but you can't do it if you don't understand marketing's multifaceted role:

- To identify, connect with, and attract the best quality and quantity of desirable prospects

- To convert these prospects into first-time buyers, upgrade them to multiple-product buyers, and compel them to return as often as they find it necessary (and desirable) to receive the absolute maximum outcome

■ To ethically mine them for alternative or ancillary revenue streams that will improve the quality of your relationship and enhance, enrich, or protect the results in their line of business

When you compare my definition of marketing with what most small-businesspeople *call* "marketing," you can see why I refer to my version as "strategic marketing," because there's a very specific plan in place to move prospects down a highly integrated progressive-growth path. Strategic marketing is designed to address the above-mentioned sequence of steps, which need to transpire in any business situation.

The marketing plans I develop are always done as profit centers. Most businesspeople believe that they can't afford to spend money on marketing. My response: If you spend money on marketing, it's not marketing. Marketing is the greatest *return-on-investment* activity a business can ever do.

Let me give you an example. Most businesspeople have a modest to extensive understanding of investing, whether it's in real estate, stocks and bonds, or options. The concept of investing is to have capital at work, earning roughly 12 to 20 percent in a good market or 5 to 7 percent (if you're lucky) in a bad market. Certainly, you never want to lose capital. If an entrepreneur could make an investment that was virtually guaranteed to return 10 to 15 percent, wouldn't that be a wise move?

Marketing is so powerful that, if done correctly, it can provide an ROI of more than 100 percent on a consistent basis, and sometimes even multiples of 100 percent or higher. Now, that's a wise investment!

Most people don't realize it, but almost every activity a business engages in is an investment with the hopes of ROI. Businesses invest in people, facilities, equipment, inventory, and training, but only because they hope that they'll turn a profit, which may come in many forms, including cost reduction and increased sales.

Let's say you have a warehouse that you then expand. The increase in square footage is meant to be a profit center; otherwise, you wouldn't have spent the extra money. The same goes for a piece of equipment. You wouldn't drop a ton of money on a new widget that you didn't think would bring you back a profit, whether it's through increased output or decreased time expenditure, less capital tied up, or whatnot.

Marketing has the capacity to bestow hundreds of percent in ROI—if you do it right. And doing it right means understanding marketing's role, then integrating it to produce a specifically desired outcome.

MARKETING AS PART OF YOUR STRATEGIC PLAN

Now that you know what marketing is and does, you need to integrate it into your overall plan. First, ask yourself this question: *What is it I want to accomplish?*

At one of my seminars, my guest speaker was a former senior instructor for the Navy SEALS. His methodology was impressive in its utter simplicity. All actions were reduced to three elements: targets, weapons, and movement. He said you couldn't be successful in an interaction if you didn't know your target, and if you had a lot of targets, you had to prioritize them. With your first target in mind, you had to choose the right weapon for maximum impact, then decide the right movement to get in range with that weapon.

The same goes for marketing. Marketing is used to target the best source of prospects and then to access them in the most cost-effective manner, which varies depending on your industry but will always involve one of the same three basic structures of business growth. I cover this topic more deeply in my first book, *Getting Everything You Can Out of All You've Got*, but the abbreviated version is that there are only three ways to grow any business:

1. Increase your client/base.

2. Increase the amount of each transaction.

3. Increase the frequency of transactions.

Let's say you're a business owner making $100,000 a year and that your goal is to make $1 million. If you maintain the same business model you're currently using, the only way to reach your goal is to do ten times the business. But that's a difficult proposition because it requires much more capital, personnel, and infrastructure, and perhaps a different management skill set than you alone currently have.

So, after you set your goal, you identify the more expedient, leverageable, alternative ways to get there. For example, you might make the same transactions twice as profitable, which would mean you'd need only five times your current number of transactions to hit your goals. You could work on getting your clients to return more often, or introduce a new product that adds ten times the profit (or many times more ongoing purchases), which would accomplish your goal in one fell swoop.

The point is, there are a lot of different ways to do it, but it's not actually doable until you first clearly define the goal and know why you want to reach it. If you identify the higher, better-performing, alternative methods available, you'll get there faster and stay there longer.

And what's the key to doing this? Marketing, of course.

HOW TO DEVELOP YOUR STRATEGIC MARKETING PLAN: FOLLOW THE MAVEN MATRIX

Because strategic marketing is so important, my friend and collaborator Rich Schefren and I came up with the Maven Matrix to help spell out the secrets for success. Below are nine steps that will teach you how to market like a millionaire. And if you follow these steps, you just might become one.

Step #1: Gain Your Market's Trust

We are now living in a copycat world where, in the wake of the voracious demons of marginalizing and commoditizing, most products and services all look alike. The marketing matches the décor—almost everyone's conventional marketing messages seem exactly the same. No one stands out as really being the supreme choice. Your prospects and clients can't tell who is really competent, who has their best interests at heart, and who they can and should trust with their purchasing decisions and all future purchases.   .

As a result, they rely on expert advisers, friends, and what's already familiar to guide them in their purchasing decisions. But this blurring of differentiation, this replicating of one mundane marketing message after another, is actually an enormous *opportunity*. It's an opportunity because it allows you the chance—ignored by 99.9 percent of other people in your field—to assume the preeminent role in your market.

You can almost instantly install yourself as your market's dominant go-to source by doing one simple thing: *caring more*. If you can show your prospects what they should be doing differently to solve their problems, fill their needs, or achieve their goals, you've just begun the process of winning their trust. And if they trust you, they will look to you for advice and purchasing solutions for their problems. Again, it all starts with empathy.

We talked about empathy in Chapter 5, but not specifically about how it pertains to marketing. Empathy is one of your most valuable tools when the time comes to market your products or services, because it allows you to persuade your clients with the maximum impact and efficiency.

If you don't know your market's "pain point," you're probably marginalizing your results. So employ the market research techniques we explored in Chapter 4, and once you've got a list of pain points, synthesize them into a blanket statement. Even better, weave them into a personal story of your own that illustrates your understanding of the market's frustrations. When your target audience can see themselves in your story, you've just secured their attention. More on that later.

For now, let's break the process down step by step. First, describe the biggest problems confronting the people in your market, and the frustrations that come along with them. Then, put your list of problems and frustrations into chronological order. Determine which problem usually comes first (or is most important to the majority), what problem usually follows that, and so on until your list is sequenced from first problem to last.

Next, come up with at least three ways to articulate these problems better than your prospects have been able to. It's not as hard as it might sound; nobody else is making the effort to come up with better ways to describe problems, so taking the time to think about such things will give you a huge advantage here. Why? Because it telegraphs to your prospects that you acknowledge what they are dealing with.

With the prospects' problems laid out clearly in front of you, you are now free to craft the best way to solve them. If you feel stuck getting started, here's an example to give you a better perspective.

Remember Jim Cook, the "Rare Coin Maven" from Chapter 8? Here's how he empathizes with his marketplace:

"It's smart for investors to be worried about rampant inflation and to be concerned about now knowing how to invest in hard money, like gold and silver coins. But you need to be careful because practically every other gold and silver coin dealer out there uses high-pressure sales tactics and tries to get you to make big commitments right up front because their plan is to churn your account. I'd rather you start small, and get comfortable first."

Identifying a prospect's pain is about being specific, detailed, and straightforward with your client base. That's how you gain the trust of your market.

Step #2: Establish Your Preeminent, Proprietary Maven Persona

We talked about the three P's in Chapter 8; now's the time to translate them into action.

Translation is actually a good metaphor, because we're about to get a little literary. In his book *Leading Minds: An Anatomy of Leadership,* Harvard professor Howard Gardner wrote, "Leaders achieve effectiveness largely through the stories they relate. Stories must in some way help audience/team members to think through who they are and frame future opinions." We'll talk more about writing your own story in a moment. For now, let's focus on another novelistic aspect of marketing: character.

Preeminent businesspeople are market leaders who are trusted—at least in part because they have secured their piece of mental "real estate" in the market. In other words, their targeted prospects and clients feel as though they know them. The question for you, then, is this: How do thousands of people whom you never met get to know *you*? How do they come to at least feel as if they know you personally? This is where the secrets, methods, strategies, and techniques of personal branding come into play. In a marketing context, people can get to know you only through the *consistent* character role or persona that you project through your communications.

Unfortunately, most businesspeople project absolutely no character persona to the market. Change that one element alone, and your positive marketing impact will skyrocket.

A persona isn't a fabrication. Rather, it's a distillation—a public presentation, so to speak—that allows you to communicate your essential beliefs, values, and standards in an efficient way. An effective maven character persona combines the elements of your own personality (your own strengths and, sometimes, even weaknesses) with those traits that resonate most effectively with your market.

Some TV shows, movies, and novels become blockbusters, whereas others simply bomb, for reasons having largely to do with the *characters* involved. Think Columbo, House, Gill Grissom on *CSI*, Rocky, Rambo, Harrison Ford in *Indiana Jones*, or Matt Damon as Jason Bourne. In the entertainment world, it's common knowledge that if the market doesn't connect with the characters in a TV show, film, or novel, they will never sell well. In fact, if audiences like the characters, they will often tolerate a lot of negatives, like poor plots or substandard special effects. Think about this the next time you see a movie or read a novel. What types of characters are you attracted to, and why? At the same time, think about what types of characters your clients and prospects like and most positively relate to.

Few entrepreneurs have any clue about this. But whether people are sitting in a dark movie theater with a bag of popcorn or looking to invest in a multimillion-dollar corporation, they are attracted to certain kinds of characters. It follows logically that you have to create a character for your business that people will like and trust. You have to reveal aspects of your personality and share with the public who you are. The more successfully you do this, the likelier it will be that people feel they know and trust you—and the faster your business will grow.

I'm not advocating phoniness. Quite the opposite. But the truth is, a human being is a complex reality with many facets that can't easily be communicated in e-mails, newspaper ads, or brief online videos. Accordingly, you have to select those character traits and stances that most accurately reflect who you are and what you are attempting to achieve in your market.

Just to be clear, I am not suggesting that you send your clients and prospects an e-mail or letter containing your complete bio. Rather, my point is that you must make yourself known the same way an author makes a character known: through your behavior. And, indeed, the best way to get clients, prospects, and the overall market to feel as though they know you is by sharing stories that portray you as behaving congruently with the persona you've chosen and defined. In a similar vein, writing instructors advise: "Show, don't tell." A character description describes what kind of person your character is. But the story must also *demonstrate* what kind of person he or she is.

One final note from the world of fiction: You'll be more believable if you're not perfect. A useful flaw in your character makes you more interesting and gives you a hook so that you penetrate deeply into the minds of your marketplace. The marketplace then sees you as human and real.

By researching our respective client files, Rich and I identified more than twenty-four common character types. These categories can be found in almost any market or niche. I've included some of the main ones on the next couple pages. Don't think of this as a definitive list; the truth is, there are as many preeminent personas as there are unique individuals—an infinite number. If one of these types resonates with you, use it; but you can also create your own or mix and match different personas to come up with a unique hybrid. This process is like being at the buffet table of business success: You simply pick the parts that are right for you and your market.

Typical Character Types: Which One Are You?

- *The Confident Tycoon or Big-Business Builder.* Often a worka-holic, this character is always looking for the next big deal. He's a visionary but sometimes runs the risk of coming across as conceited or arrogant. We all know the type—it's Donald Trump.

- *The Puppeteer Behind the Scenes*—or Henry Kissinger, in a nut-shell. Calculated and mysterious, this character works in the shadows. Everyone knows the Puppeteer is powerful (or rich, or smart, or any other trait), but no one is exactly sure how he or she actually operates.

- *The Researcher.* This character is curious and hard-working, and often an impulsive finder of truth. Steve Wozniak of Apple Com-puters, who is known for his introversion, embodies the core characteristics of this type.

- *The Well-Placed Intelligence Source.* The Source is the one who shows you what's happening behind the scenes. People of this type are confrontational and demanding, with very high standards. They are typically determined and forceful, organized and disciplined. Bill O'Reilly is the prime example.

- *The "Self-Made" Man or Woman.* This is someone like the bil-lionaire Carl Icahn or Meg Whitman of eBay. Determined and persistent, Self-Made characters are very proud of their accom-plishments. They generally have high expectations of others; they're the corporate raider or takeover type.

- *The Contrarian.* When I imagine a Contrarian personality type, I think of Sam Zell, who sold all his real estate and bought the

Tribune editorial empire (which publishes the *Chicago Tribune* and the *Los Angeles Times* newspapers). People of this type are distrustful of any big system (whether governmental or corporate). They often believe in conspiracies, and although they're generally well-read, they may be a little on the fringe.

■ *The Eccentric.* These characters make their own rules, and they hate to be lumped in with the rest of the group and value their uniqueness above all else. The Eccentric can be counted on to be generous, animated, unconventional, and adventurous— Richard Branson of Virgin Airlines comes to mind.

■ *The Iconoclast* is not concerned with tradition. Like John G. Sperling, founder of the University of Phoenix, the Iconoclast has little respect for authority unless such respect is well-deserved. These characters are defined by their willingness to take risks.

■ *The Angry Man.* We all know someone like this: the red-faced character, like Jim Cramer of *Mad Money*. Argumentative and self-righteous, the Angry Man is an excitable and sometimes amusing insider.

■ *The Prodigy/Genius.* Introverted and super-intelligent, the Prodigy is confident and aggressive. These characters are sometimes condescending and frequently socially inept. Can you say "Bill Gates"?

■ *The Fun Guy.* This person is the life of the party: Terry Bradshaw and Charles Barkley are the obvious examples here. Such characters are optimistic and happy; they see the good in situations. They're good at raising people's spirits, and their enthusiasm is contagious.

You probably get the idea by now. So, as an exercise, list some personality traits for each of the remaining types:

■ *The Synthesizer* (Tony Robbins)

■ *The Outcast* (Jeff Katzenberg of SKG)

■ *The Common Man* (Howard Stern)

■ *The Intellect* (Newt Gingrich)

■ *The Advocate* (Paul Newman)

■ *The Mad Scientist* (Jeong Kim of Bell Labs)

■ *The Supreme Possibility-Optimist* (Zig Ziglar)

■ *The Futurist* (John Nasbit, Faith Popcorn)

■ *The Absent-Minded Professor* (Albert Einstein)

■ *The Wizard* (Steve Jobs)

■ *The Family Man* (John Chambers of Cisco)

Okay, at this point it's time to think about your own pre-eminent persona. Ask yourself how that persona could be improved, dimensionalized, refined, or redefined. Imagine a famous Hollywood actor playing you in a big-budget movie. Which actor would get the job? How would he or she act? What would the story be about? How would viewers describe the character? Now think about what type of characters/personas would score high in your market. Which personality types are they attracted to? Which types do they find easy to like? Which character persona "voids" are waiting to be filled?

Remember, establishing your character persona affords the opportunity to have a little fun. Highlight the best parts of yourself, and bring other optimal parts to the surface. This is your chance to be who you've always wanted to be. As Isabel Allende said, "You are the storyteller of your own life, and you can create your own legend or not."

Step #3: Develop a Vision for Your Marketplace

Once you've created a preeminent persona that both matches your personal strengths and resonates with your market, the next step is to develop and clearly state the elements of your market vision—the core beliefs that will guide your service to your market. Here are just three examples; many more could be listed.

- Fred Smith of Federal Express developed his vision of reliable overnight document delivery anywhere in America. His slogan is known far and wide: "When it absolutely, positively has to be there overnight."

- Tom Monahan developed his vision of the way pizza delivery should be and turned it into a slogan and a promise: "Hot pizza in 30 minutes or it's free."

- Larry Page and Sergey Brin developed their vision of a search engine for the Internet that could quickly retrieve the most relevant web pages and started their company in a friend's garage in 1998. Within a decade of its launch, Google was worth an estimated $23 billion.

Unfortunately, many entrepreneurs focus not on a vision for their market but, instead, on their businesses. They fall in love with their own products, with their service, or with the notion of being the fastest-growing company in the field. However, as I've said before, the key to rapid success as a preeminent business is *to fall in love with your clients.* If you can really live for the benefit, the advantage, the enrichment, the protection, and the interaction you create in their lives, you'll achieve preeminence quickly.

So dig down deep, and find a real and purposeful reason for your company to exist.

Step #4: Tell Your Creation Myth

Writer and researcher of group dynamics Christina Baldwin once said, "Words are how we think, story is how we link." Preeminent businesspeople have a story, a personal history, and a track record with their market. Their success depends upon how well they communicate it. You have to tell the world *why* you're in the market you're in. You have to reveal your hopes and dreams, your current frustrations, your personal failures, what you've achieved so far, and what you're still struggling to achieve. Do that, with honesty and passion, and you'll achieve success beyond anything you could ever expect. Fail to do that—become just one among hundreds of also-ran, "me-too" businesses—and you'll become a commodity, forever cutting your prices.

Author and international keynote speaker Tom Peters puts it this way: "He who has the best story, wins." It's that simple. Think about the classic maven stories we've all heard. There's the one about Bill Gates, who shrewdly purchased an operating system (86-DOS) from a Seattle software company and then licensed it to IBM as the operating system for its new PC. Or the one about Phil Knight, the University of Oregon track star who began experimenting with a waffle iron to make his own running shoes. The company he founded, Nike, ended up bequeathing him a personal fortune of $9 billion. And by now, of course, everyone knows the story of Steve Jobs and Steve Wozniak, who, in a Menlo Park garage, put together a personal computer that became the Apple.

Companies thrive on the basis of the stories they tell. How do we know the stories about Bill Gates and Steve Jobs—or Mark Zuckerberg of Facebook and Robin Chase of Zipcar? Because they have told them over and over again. Mavens, above all else, tell stories. These personal narratives provide explanations of why they do what they do—which, in turn, indicate why their clients and prospects should trust them.

When I use the term "creation myth," I don't mean "myth" in the sense that something is being made up. Rather, my intent is to evoke the lovely, lyrical notion of a tale as old as time; a story of origin, history, and purpose. Think back to how you found your way into your market in the first place. What drew you to it? If you just stumbled into it, what kept you there? What do you like about your market? What do you dislike? Go even deeper. Think about your greatest achievements in this market. Then think about your greatest failures. Use this process as a way to be honest. A truthful "I feel your pain" story can be an incredibly effective tool for connecting with your market. The more honest you are, the more you will gain your market's trust—and the more trust you have, the more you can ethically advise prospects on what they should buy.

Step #5: Become a Polarizing Figure

Adlai Stevenson is said to have once unfavorably compared his own oratory to President Kennedy's by saying "In classical times, when Cicero had finished speaking, the people said, 'How well he spoke.' But when Demosthenes had finished speaking, they said, 'Let us march.'"

Part of standing for something is standing against something else. Successful mavens are often polarizing: They announce to the world that clients should not tolerate certain low standards of service, shoddy products, misleading advertising, and the people and businesses that practice them. In other words, successful mavens usually have a strong point of view.

After all, people flock to them to hear their opinions of the market niche they are in—and the more direct and passionate those opinions are, the more they resonate with the market. Such pronouncements needn't be negative; mavens don't have to "name names" in order to be heard. But they should definitely defend the interests of their clients and prospects by denouncing what needs to be denounced. Here's an example.

Chase Revell was a hard-nosed businessman who went from project to project. I discovered that Chase had spent his whole adult life studying business trends that became huge moneymakers. He was also opinionated. He called things like he saw them. He praised some companies and denounced others. So I used this polarizing quality to help position Chase as preeminent. Together, we created a report titled "Who's Making a Bundle?" The report highlighted Chase as a no-nonsense guy who didn't waste a moment of his time on anything less than the absolute highest payoff for the least amount of time; it also revealed that he had done the research and had a tough-businessman perspective unlike that of anyone else.

That preeminent positioning, combined with skilled marketing techniques, catapulted Chase's business into the stratosphere. The name of his business is *Entrepreneur* magazine—now an international publishing conglomerate with hundreds of millions in sales. When done right, taking strong, polarizing opinions will win you followers (as well as enemies) and create monster levels of financial success.

So think of yourself as a reformer. If you were a client in your market, what would you change? How would you improve things? What's wrong? What's needed? What's missing? If you could address a professional association in your market, what would you say? What would you demand? With your superior knowledge of your market, how would you advise inexperienced prospects? Launch a consumer crusade.

Step #6: Develop Your Own Phraseology

When you're preeminent, people feel as though they know who you are. And part of knowing someone is being able to anticipate certain traits. That's why successful mavens develop what are known as "rituals" or predictable behaviors that clients come to expect and even look forward to.

One way to do this is to develop a unique style of communicating. Charles Dickens used this technique more than a century ago. When creating his characters, Dickens gave each one a unique verbal tic—a special phrase or accent or way of beginning a sentence—so that readers could instantly figure out who was speaking. Of course, Dickens wasn't the first to do this, and he was by no means the last. Here are two contemporary examples.

Internet marketer Matt Furey sells wrestling and health products on www .mattfurey.com. Furey's e-mails are filled with odd spellings (e.g., "nekkid"), which, along with his trademark ending, "Kick Butt—Take Names," play up his sassy point of view. In a different vein, Warren Buffett's annual reports are anticipated and read by more people than actually own Berkshire-Hathaway stock.

My point is that to solidify your relationship with your market, you, too, should develop certain ritualistic behaviors that your clients and prospects can predict. These will allow them to feel as though they know you. And the more predictable you are, the more people will come to trust you.

Mavens are market leaders, experts, and authorities in their fields. As such, they define the terms of the debate, set the standards, and engineer the solutions. In your own capacity as a maven, you would develop your own "technology," your unique phraseology and ways of presenting your understanding.

It's a simple concept: Take certain words and make them yours. Tony Robbins is a classic example of this.

Tony Robbins was trained in Neuro-Linguistic Programming (NLP). He modified some of the conditions slightly and renamed it Neuro-Associated Conditioning (NAC). He took another concept and called it the "Dickens Pattern." And based on an additional quality concept from Ed Deming, he created his own, proprietary acronym, which was CANI (Constant and Never-Ending Improvement).

Rich Schefren has done something similar. He used the term "manifesto" when writing his foundational business report, and to this day, if you speak to anyone in Internet marketing circles and you say, "I'm looking for the Manifesto," people will naturally assume you're talking about Rich. Another phrase that he coined for a whole series of reports was "doctrine." His last report was called *The Attention Age Doctrine*. "Doctrine" sounds crucially important, as if it is the *only* text on a given subject—so important that no client in his right mind would want to miss it.

The truth is, you can take any phrase or term and make it your own. *The Attention Age Doctrine* was also known for its initial use of the phrase "Attention Age." Rich emphasized that *attention* has become a scarce commodity, although he wasn't the first person to talk about this; a Nobel Prize–winning scientist mentioned it in 1971 (the year Rich was born). But Rich created the term "Attention Age" and made it his own. Today, if you check on Google, there's something like 100,000 web pages that talk about our being in the Attention Age—and the majority of those pages cite Rich as the maven who coined the term.

So, pretend for a moment that you're not merely the preeminent authority in your market but an actual pioneer, a scientist, an explorer. You've been given the task of explaining the intricacies of your market to beginners—of telling them what they need to know and why. Now pretend that you actually have to create your own system to explain the market. Develop your own terminology, your own system, your own explanatory hypothesis. Imagine that you're writing a book or an e-book on your market. What would you say? Could you find new words, new phrases, to describe different aspects of the products or services in your market? Could you organize your market better than it's now organized? Could you prioritize better? Value things better?

Step #7: Use a Signature Communications Channel

Part of developing rituals in your business is to use a signature communication channel, a special way of communicating with your marketplace that is unique to you, whether it's a Monday-morning e-mail, a blog, a video podcast, or a monthly newsletter. Here's an example.

Gary Vaynerchuk uses an inexpensive, low-tech video blog to communicate with his followers. He does daily five- to fifteen-minute videos about wine enjoyment for the average Joe. He's a perfect example of an "ordinary" businessman using the power of preeminence to get exponential results—and very quickly.

Gary is about as regular a guy as you'll ever meet. He grew up in New Jersey and helped out in the family business, a modest liquor store. But Gary saw an opportunity to become a maven in a particular niche of his market. He saw that a lot of his clients were interested in and wanted to buy more expensive wines, but they didn't know much about wine. Fine wine, they felt, was for snobs.

So what did Gary do? He launched his very inexpensive video blog, www.winelibrarytv.com, which features his outrageous, sometimes profane but always-hilarious commentaries on wine. By catering to and championing this underserved market (ordinary wine drinkers as opposed to wine connoisseurs), Gary has transformed his family's once-small neighborhood liquor store into a $50 million company using this mechanism.

Gary is now a maven. He's "the" expert on wine for the average person. He's been on *The Conan O'Brien* show, *The Ellen DeGeneres* show, and many others. In fact, he's gotten so much attention recently, he now has an agent. He has already received offers from TV networks and major cable stations that want him to host his own show. If you ever hear someone say that being preeminent isn't for "ordinary businesses," tell them about Gary Vaynerchuk.

Step #8: Create a Velvet Rope Community

William James said, "The deepest human need is the need to be appreciated." Becoming preeminent means being seen as the servant-leader of a community. Mavens deliberately create communities by providing their clients and prospects with value-laden information, opinions, and advice. Rather than wasting precious resources on mass advertising that clients deliberately avoid at all costs, savvy mavens use sophisticated strategies to engage consumers in active conversations about a given marketplace. Conventional advertising is nothing more than a monologue—and frequently a rude and rather loud one at that. Preeminent marketing, in contrast, is a *dialogue*.

By serving your market and putting the needs of your clients above your own profit, you can demonstrate to the marketplace that they can and should be treated like VIPs— that they should get what I call the "velvet rope" treatment. Cultivate the unique habit of treating people like relevant, important people, not mere clients. That is the psychology behind the velvet rope.

Anyone who has ever gone clubbing knows, or can imagine, what it's like to receive VIP treatment. Other people stand in line for hours, hoping to be allowed into the club and allowed to pay the large cover charge. But imagine if you could just step up to the velvet rope, be instantly recognized as a celebrity or VIP, and then get whisked past the lines of ordinary people into the elite inner sanctum of the club. You'd feel like a million bucks, right?

That is what it should feel like to be a client of a preeminent company. It treats its clients like VIPs, inviting them to higher and higher levels of service, special treatment, and quality. Here's a great example of that type of service.

Brian owned a tiny health company selling an arthritis product called Icy-Hot. When I first started working with Brian, company sales were tiny—about $20,000 in sales revenues from that product. But by repositioning Brian as the *champion* of the arthritis-inflicted masses, we helped him create a trusting, caring relationship with his clients that attracted more than 500,000 people to buy from him.

The preeminent strategy I implemented was based on building unbreakable client loyalty. It worked because 80 percent of first-time Icy-Hot buyers repurchased *twelve times or more a year*. The result: Brian went from $20,000 in sales to $13 million in a single year. He then sold his company for 8 figures—that's right, for more than a billion dollars!—to a large pharmaceutical conglomerate.

I used the little-known techniques of preeminent branding to help create a business persona for Brian. The truth is, Brian was a very fit 40-year-old man. But when I created ads for him, I used a stock photo of a 70-year-old, somewhat cherub-faced fellow, so readers could identify with someone having sensitivity and understanding for sufferers of arthritis. The ads and letters had headlines that read "I want you to have blessed relief." They painted the picture of a maven who had studied all the treatments—presumably for his own relief—and found one that was as old as could be.

Brian created so much empathetic connection with people that clients actually wrote loving, appreciative fan letters. They felt understood, valued, just like VIP members of a private club—except that, in this case, the club was made up of people who had arthritis. Brian became not just a successful health-product salesman but a champion of arthritis sufferers worldwide—their hero. His clients were not merely clients. Instead, they became lifelong, loyal friends.

Take a moment to imagine your ideal client. Picture him or her in your mind. Someone who raves about your products or services. Someone who repurchases from you over and over again. Now, think about what you would do for such a client. How would you treat him or her? If you knew your dream client would make you X amount of money each year, how much of that money would you be willing to spend to keep him or her happy?

This is what I call the *lifetime value* of a client. Once you know what individual clients are worth to you over the long term, you know how much to spend or "invest" to acquire them—and how much to spend to keep them deliriously happy. Your sales will explode—and you will develop an enormous following of clients who will remain loyal for life.

Once you've successfully created a velvet rope community, you should have no trouble transforming your loyal clients into client evangelists. Research shows that consumers today make most of their important decisions by seeking the advice of an expert or of a trusted friend. Word of mouth is growing in importance. When people tune out conventional marketing, they turn to social networks for purchasing advice; in fact, the best indicator of future sales growth is the number of "client-evangelists" a business has. So, the more people who recommend your products or services, the more likely your sales will grow.

With modern life becoming increasingly advanced and complex, many people assume it simply takes too long to make the right decision all by themselves. That's why prospects put so much trust in people willing to help them solve their problems. Mavens take ethical advantage of this reality and leverage it for enormous success. By raising the bar of quality, service, or care far above what anyone can legitimately expect, they create a natural "wow" factor that itself builds buzz.

Think of ways you can help, not merely your current clients or prospects, but their clients or prospects, their friends, their relatives—anyone they come into contact with. Think up promotions, giveaways, free reports, and advice hotlines—

anything your clients can use to help the people they know. Think "virally": How can you turn your happy clients into evangelists for your products and services, for your cause, for your vision?

Step #9: Accelerate the Process with Mentors

Many people have stumbled upon the secret of "mavenship" through trial and error. But by completing the Maven Matrix provided in this chapter, you already have an enormous advantage over most businesses. You have a blueprint that can guide you going forward. Of course it's not going to work overnight. With the insights you've gained into yourself and your business, you could spend the next several years experimenting and trying to apply the principles and steps I've described.

Fortunately, though, there's an easier, faster, result-certain way. That is to use trusted mentors and advisors, those who have already laid the foundations for hundreds of preeminent companies themselves, to help you implement each of these steps. Experienced mentors will be able to draw on your own deepest inspirations, your greatest personal strengths, and the tasks you instinctively enjoy doing to help you achieve preeminence quickly.

Whatever your field or industry, there are undoubtedly celebrities within it—big-name companies or professionals. Now, imagine you can approach these celebrities and partner with them to promote products or services in your niche. Think of the status you would instantly achieve if you could be aligned with them—whether for advice, direction, fast-tracking of your results, or endorsement. Assuming they have agreed to align themselves with your business, what would you do to create a project they would participate in with you? What resources would you need to make this happen?

The most successful people have *all* had mentors. Bob Dylan was mentored by Woody Guthrie. Richard Branson of Virgin Airlines was mentored by Freddie Laker, who founded Laker Airways, the first low-cost airline to fly between London and New York. Amazon founder Jeff Bezos was mentored by David Shaw, founder of a hedge fund that *Fortune* described as "the most intriguing and mysterious force on Wall Street." Warren Buffett was mentored by economist Benjamin Graham, the author of the investment classic *Security Analysis*. And there's no reason you shouldn't have one, too.

The process of becoming a maven is like releasing the parking brake on a new Porsche. Once you remove the self-defeating behaviors and subtle acts of self-sabotage that businesspeople routinely inflict on their own marketing efforts, business becomes a joy—more like play than work. And that joy starts multiplying geometrically. In fact, the more fun you're having, the quicker your success will come—and the bigger your financial rewards.

PUTTING YOUR MAVEN MATRIX TO WORK

So, what does it mean to put the Maven Matrix into action? Here are some real-life stories of businesses that dared to move beyond mediocre marketing into the world beyond.

In the early 1990s, I worked with a prominent Beverly Hills cosmetic surgeon. Back then, he and all his local competitors were timid about their marketing. I convinced him to offer a free sixty-minute promotional video to prospects. He ran ads offering the video in the *Los Angeles Times*, *Los Angeles Magazine*, and the L.A. editions of *Cosmopolitan* and *Vogue*. Up to that point, no one else in his profession knew how to market using a sophisticated, tasteful, educational infomercial. As a result, he built a monster practice.

Marketing can also be used for something other than cash flow. Years ago, while running *Entrepreneur* magazine, my associates and I were engaged in seven parallel marketing functions; one of these involved creating and selling memberships to an exclusive subscriber-like newsletter. The newsletter staff's primary job was to produce a monthly twenty- to thirty-page research report on emerging small-business enterprises, opportunities, and investment situations.

On the last day of each month, when the issue of the membership newsletter became outdated, we would add another twenty to thirty pages of timely information from different industries, thus creating multiple versions that we then sold for $39 each as start-up manuals. Each year, that newly packaged report brought in roughly 7 to 8 million dollars—almost 80 percent pure profit—even though the newsletter publishing division that created those reports barely broke even. So the same product was used both for maintaining our subscriber base and for producing our revenue-generating reports.

Harnessing marketing's capabilities is a matter of believing that your job as an entrepreneur is to make your business work harder and harder for you, so that you can work less and less for it. The harder your business works, the more asset value it creates, too.

Unfortunately, a lot of businesspeople default to traditional marketing instead of trying new things, which actually makes their job harder. They run semi-institutional-type ads (rather than direct-responsive ones) or have a sales team that makes cold calls. They don't think beyond the conventional methods they've seen their whole lives. Here, on the other hand, are some examples of truly creative marketing techniques.

Just recently, I held an entrepreneurial fact-finding session with a group of dentists. Our goal was to hear alternative methods that practices had used to build their successful client base. Some doctors were slogging it out the old-fashioned way with advertising and Yellow Pages, but a few had hit on some truly revolutionary ideas. One doctor produced a traveling puppet show for schools that was seen by as many as 4,000 children a month, which in turn generated 100 to 150 new cases, at an average of $1,500 annually apiece.

Another doctor went the philanthropic route, offering teeth-whitening services, valued at $300 each, free to anyone who donated to a high school scholarship fund. The treatment cost the dentist $50 to fulfill, whereas he determined that cold leads from ads and Yellow Pages generally cost $150 (in other words, three times more) to generate. Many teeth-whitening clients became $2,000-a-year patients, translating into an overall gain of nearly $200,000 per year for the dentist—all from that simple-sounding nontraditional approach.

Another dentist I worked with sent any client who referred a new patient to him a written thank-you note—along with a lottery ticket. Talk about a failsafe, creative method of establishing a relationship with your clients!

Here's a fourth example of using creative marketing to generate referrals and more business: A car dealer started sending helium-filled balloons to his customers at work after they bought a car from him. The balloons had no advertising on them, but they would float above the customers' chairs while they worked. Their co-workers, in turn, would think somebody was having a birthday and ask them about it, and pretty soon the customers would be bragging about their new car and what a great experience they'd had at the dealership. Within nine months of starting this practice, the dealer's business from referral clients had increased 50 percent.

With the Maven Matrix as your guide, you, too, can put these lessons to work. This is your chance to revolutionize your marketing strategy. The possibilities are just waiting to be discovered.

I have no formal secondary education, but I can tell you that most universities teach only theoretical marketing, not the sound, practical, result-based kind I'm putting forth here. My education was earned in the trenches, on the front lines of real capitalism, dealing firsthand with entrepreneurs who didn't have the luxury of wasting time and money. They had to make *every* marketing activity a profit center. With a small amount of capital they had to produce big results.

Your days of mediocre marketing are over. Now you know how to market like a maven, and you can keep returning to the nine specific steps of the Maven Matrix to get you there. Apply these lessons to your business, and you'll reap a windfall of rewards.

There's only one last thing you need to know to get your business unstuck, and it's this: You can't go it alone. If you want to know why, turn to the next chapter.

The Bottom Line

■ Redefine the word "marketing" for yourself as the process of educating the marketplace. Inform your potential clients that your business can solve problems, fill voids, or achieve opportunities and goals in a way that no other business can.

■ One objective of marketing's role in your business is to identify, connect with, and attract the best quality and quantity of desirable prospects.

■ A second objective is to convert your prospects to first-time buyers, upgrade them to multiple-product buyers, and compel them to return as often as necessary for them to receive the absolute maximum outcome.

■ A third objective is to ethically mine your prospects for alternative revenue streams that will improve the quality of your relationship and enhance their lives.

■ Think of marketing as an investment, but one so powerful it can provide an ROI of more than 100 percent on a consistent basis—and sometimes even multiples of 100 percent.

- You can't reach your goal until you define it. *What is it you want to accomplish?*

- Follow the nine steps of the Maven Matrix: Gain your market's trust, establish a persona, develop a vision for your marketplace, tell your story, become a polarizing figure, develop your own phraseology, use a signature communications channel, create a velvet rope community, and work with mentors.

☞ **Immediate Action Step** Bill Clinton is remembered for the phrase "I feel your pain." Take out a sheet of paper and write down the top three pains your clients and prospects feel. Keep this list in plain sight at all times, as your business will grow to the extent that you feel—and can articulate—the pain your clients and prospects feel.

10

ARE YOU STUCK STILL SAYING "I CAN DO IT MYSELF"?

Ask any business owners you know whether they invest in their company's 401(k) plan and the answer, invariably, will be "Of course!" Then ask them what kind of return on their 401(k) would really knock their socks off. They'll probably tell you that 10 percent would be amazing, and that—in their wildest fantasies—they dream of getting 14 percent.

My response would be this: Even 14 percent would be anemic compared to the return on investment of hiring someone to create joint ventures for you. When you learn and understand the science of leveraging the talents of others, your resulting return will dwarf any passive investment you could ever hope to make.

At heart, entrepreneurism is all about leveraging people, assets, capital, and efforts. It's about helping other people get what they want so they'll give and get you everything *you* want. As Robert Hargrove has pointed out, the most defining trait of great entrepreneurs in the twenty-first century will be the ability to creatively collaborate with other people, because individual business professionals could never acquire all of the necessary skills themselves.

In this chapter, I want to shake you out of the "control freak" mode of insisting on doing everything yourself. I want you to dispel the idea that no one else can be trusted or that no one else can do the job as well. If that's your attitude, your business won't last long, and it certainly won't return the level of geometric growth you're hoping for. Failing to leverage means condemning your business to a lifetime of stagnation.

As I mentioned way back in Chapter 2, there's good leverage and bad leverage, just as there's good and bad cholesterol:

- *Good* leverage occurs when businesspeople buy vehicles or equipment, hire new people, or move into new facilities with the goal of producing a predictable, calculable amount of ROI.

- *Bad* leverage occurs when businesspeople do the same things, only instead of knowing how much ROI the activities will produce, they only *hope* that their decisions will pay off—which, under such conditions, rarely happens. Then, instead of profit, the leverage leads to either debt service or capital diminishment.

Good leverage recycles previous buyers, helps current buyers buy more, and provides for new marketing avenues heretofore unexplored. And yet most entrepreneurs and executives invariably choose bad leverage. Don't let that happen to you.

So without much further ado, let's delve into how you can get on the right side of the good leverage/bad leverage equation.

KNOWING WHEN TO STAY PUT AND *NOT* EXPAND YOUR BUSINESS

Entrepreneurs say, "We have to get our sales up, so we need to hire more salespeople." However, what I have personally witnessed is that for every salesperson brought in, businesses frequently lose as much as 20 cents on the dollar. Obviously, that's bad leverage—hiring new salespeople accelerated the rate at which the businesses lost money. A better idea would be to keep the same number of staff you have now and invest in high upside-leverage "performance enhancement" training, which would result in those same employees becoming as much as 50 to 100 percent more effective. Now, that's a handsome profit!

It's the optimization versus innovation debate again. Remember: Try optimization first. Work with what you have to make it work better. Once you've trained your team in consultative advisory sales methods, *then* you can think about recruiting more salespeople, because you'll be incorporating them into a high-leverage system proven to work many times better than before you turbocharged it.

Entrepreneurs are, by nature, control freaks. The secret to your success is to realize ultimate control by shifting into the role of the benevolent puppet master. Think of P. T. Barnum—he wasn't the clown, he wasn't the trapeze artist, he wasn't the daredevil shot out of the cannon. But he masterfully orchestrated everything. He leveraged all his employees into a cohesive fabric. He gave them the spotlight, and doing that gave him the lion's share of the money.

Most entrepreneurs never give themselves the opportunity to be in a position where they can think strategically. But that's what you need to do if you really want to get unstuck. By juggling too many different roles, you're not following the concept of highest and best use. And you almost always get forced to function tactically and suboptimally.

If you're stuck in a snow bank, persisting in moving forward will only drive you in deeper and deeper. You need leverage—either people pushing from behind (collaboration) or a piece of cardboard under the tire for traction (innovation).

You can do any number of things to get yourself out, but first you have to take a good look at your options to be sure they're going to get you back on the road instead of buried deeper in snow. If they aren't, you need a new set of approaches that will accomplish the goal.

KNOWING WHEN TO EXPAND YOUR BUSINESS

It's impossible to be on the cutting edge of every area of your business—technology, sales, marketing, management, and so on. You just can't do it. The only possible way to succeed is to first acknowledge which areas you're lacking in, then to find the best person for each of those areas, and then figure out the most practical way to enlist their participation, whether it's hiring them, joint venturing with them, or trading them a service or product. The combined result of their pooled expertise, resources, and access will make for a business that thrives far beyond its competitors. If you don't have the capital to compensate them outright, you can create a collaborative relationship, such as bonuses received on a percentage basis, deferred compensation, a trade—or any combination of the above.

I've had many small clients who thought they had to go it alone. But doing it all themselves would have been the most self-limiting path imaginable. Instead of letting them trudge down such a treacherous path, I put these clients in touch with my resources—including distribution channels, creative marketing executives, and consultative sales trainers—who aided them in the areas in which they were deficient. The results were always stunning, with my clients seeing incredible expansion in areas where they'd previously seen very little growth. If my client didn't have capital, I worked around that by making compensation to the resource we recruited variable or deferred, or by moving it to equity or exchanges. Truth be told, lack of capital has never been a deterrent for my clients—or for me. Let me illustrate what I mean.

When I was about 20 years old, 8-track cassette tapes were still the standard. I found a company that was overloaded with prominent tapes but had no good distributor. I convinced the owners to give me control of $500,000 worth of tapes in exchange for the promise of split profits, and I took them to a popular chain of mini-marts in the Midwest. They agreed to let me put tapes into about 100 of their stores, and pretty soon I was making $1,000 a day. Yet I had invested *nothing* up front. It was just a matter of recognizing that one person's distress is another person's opportunity.

When you first meet with a prospective partner to propose a joint venture, take an assumptive role. Go in armed with your knowledge. But don't make any promises you can't guarantee.

Imagine going up to a prospect and saying, "Look, I know what you do well, but I know you don't do advertising. I know you don't have the sales force. I have a way to set that all up for you in five different distribution channels in selling areas and markets that you aren't reaching. It could be the tail that wags the dog. I am willing to set it all up, and once it's rolling, I want to split the profits with you—*after* we put money in your bank account. I have three other prospects for this venture who are probably your competitors, but you're my favorite and the one with the quality product that I think will get the most, do the most, and deliver the most. Do you want to join me, or should I go somewhere else?" Now who could refuse an offer like that?

But if you find that people are reluctant (and you might, especially on your first try), redouble your efforts. The way to deal with a refusal is . . . to *empathize*! Imagine if someone came to you with a joint-venture offer and followed up by saying, "If the tables were turned, and somebody I didn't know came to me with a proposition, even one that was that appealing, I would probably hesitate, too. I would wonder, *What's the catch? What does he know that I don't?* But when I thought about it, I'd realize that he *does* know something I don't. He knows how to deliver to the markets that are shutting me out. He knows how to dramatically enhance my yield, my revenue, and my profitability from what I can do alone."

Finally, to seal the deal, eliminate risk. Engineer a template for your prospects that tells them what they should demand from you in terms of controls. Be detailed, and offer things they might not even have thought of. This will demonstrate that you know your business and can be trusted to take the helm.

There are three things to avoid when you consider joint venturing. First (and what I see most commonly) is that businesspeople get caught up in the theory. There's a lot of economic theory about joint venturing, but nothing beats experience. I have taught this approach to literally thousands of people, but I see it implemented only a fraction of the time. It won't do you any good to know the theoretical returns you could glean from joint venturing if you don't get out there and give it a shot.

The second thing to avoid is starting out too big. You probably won't have a lot of success approaching big companies right off the bat, but you can create enormous wealth by engaging in several small joint ventures at once.

Third, don't allow yourself to be intimidated. You might not succeed the first time, but you can't allow yourself to be hindered by embarrassment. The odds of doing something meaningful perfectly the first time you try it are low, don't you think? The reality is that the worst thing that can happen is that your proposal will be rejected—but you still haven't lost anything. You only stand to gain.

Joint venturing is truly the fastest, safest, most flexible route you have. You can do it anywhere in the country or in the world; you can do it in person; you can do it by phone; you can do it by fax; you can do it by e-mail. Ask yourself this question: If you can bring economic advantage to clients who never had it before, and *you do all the work*, but they stand to gain $10,000, $20,000, $30,000, $50,000 a year, a quarter, a week to their bottom line, how many people do you think are going to turn down that opportunity?

CHANGING YOUR MINDSET ABOUT DOING EVERYTHING YOURSELF

As I emphasized earlier, to create opportunity you must first break free of the "go it alone" mindset and learn to move past fear to enjoy the adventure of business. Once you realize that there's always someone who has what you're lacking (and who needs what you have: vision, clarity, a plan of action), you'll never feel that fear again. It will fade away like a bad dream, and you'll forge ahead in growing your business as never before. But you have to take that leap of faith and move past your fear to be able to see what possibilities will put you on the pathway to greater prosperity. Let me share an example.

A client who owned a national franchise of educational centers insisted on doing everything himself—from approving the ads to performing the quality-control checks to training the new instructors. I taught him to skip the conventional marketing that he was so tightly controlling and to instead hire someone to create joint-venture opportunities. Reluctantly, he did so. This person received $60,000 in salary, plus a small amount of profit.

The result? She created twenty joint ventures in her first year for my client, leading to more than $1 million in new business.

The first mental step toward pushing past the fear involves recognition: Recognize the factor you're lacking (i.e., recognize your constraint) and realize that there's an infinite supply of that factor available for your use. Perhaps you need a sales force or an R&D team, or require more inventory or warehouse space. Most entrepreneurs struggle with nagging abstractions. Verbalizing your need is crucial, because it helps you to set up a concrete goal and then explore all the different options, opportunities, or alternatives available to achieve that goal rapidly and safely.

Next you have to break down the solution. Because this is the area where many entrepreneurs get stuck, let's run through the most common "stuck" scenarios.

If you need a talented copywriter but can't afford to pay one up front, the solution may be to work out a deal where you pay someone on the tangible results of her copy for as long as you use it. So instead of the normal $2,000 rate for writing copy, the copywriter now accepts zero up-front payment but has an open-ended possibility for earning for months, even years, to come. Over time, your copywriter's cut could amount to as much as ten times what she is used to earning in a one-time, up-front payment.

If you can't afford to hire a sales force, you can either find independent salespeople to take on your products or service, line up a noncompetitive company with strong representation in your market and form a joint venture, or locate an investor to fund a sales force with you and minimize that investor's risk by doing a trial run: hiring just one salesperson initially to prove to your investor that the sales team will produce a great payoff for them.

If you don't have distribution, you can find somebody who does and buy into his by giving him a permanent share of the profits that accrue as a result of your having plugged into his resources. Alternatively, you can seek out someone with underutilized services and make a deal to buy her excess people or delivery or production capacity on a per-transaction basis. That way, you're paying only when it's profitable, which means it's always a profit center and never an expense.

If you don't have the capital to stock a full supply of new products, you can test a few out first to determine the sell-through rate, then approach an investor with a conservative projection of returns and ask him to fund your investing purchase. Another method would be to find a manufacturer with that same product collecting dust in a warehouse and gain access to it by offering to split the profits once the product sells to your buyer. Remember Patrick Flanagan from Chapter 5? He built a multimillion-dollar company by selling rejected telephone systems that were too small for the big companies. He made a handsome profit, split it with the companies, and everyone walked away happy.

Part of an entrepreneur's fear of leverage stems from not knowing whom to partner with, which is understandable. However, you can greatly narrow the field by first clearly determining your real needs. Once you know your needs, you then identify who has the ability to address them.

In the past, researching this area was time consuming, but the Internet has made it a cakewalk. Rank your potential partners in order of where they stand within their industry. The odds that the top company in the market will show interest in doing a deal with you are very low. However, they're much higher for the companies in the middle of your list, as these generally want to grow but don't know how to do it because they don't think they have the resources. Determine what it is these middle-level companies are lacking and how you can solve their problems as they solve yours *at the same time*. By approaching your future partners with a solution to their problems, you'll get what you want every time—but only if you can give them what they want in exchange. Discovering your future partners' needs is a difficult skill to master, but once you've done so, it yields incalculable results. Here's an example that follows up on a story I told in Chapter 2.

Remember how I convinced a Krugerrand minter to foot my client's marketing bill? The client was a brokerage firm whose owners were dealing in rare gold and silver coins. I helped them move away from their tactical approach to doing business, which resulted in one-time-only sales. Instead, I developed a strategy that allowed them to build long-term relationships with their own clients, so that their purchases slowly increased in value as their trust in the broker increased. This meant that they were ultimately purchasing high-priced Krugerrands (back when these were legal). I was able to use this as a leverage point with the Krugerrand minter my client purchased from. Specifically, I convinced the minter to cover the brokerage firm owners' marketing expenses because I already understood their problem: They wanted to sell more Krugerrands. I knew that this was their goal. All I had to do was approach them with a viable solution—a solution that only I could provide, and one I'd already validated with a small, safe test involving ads. The minter was happy to foot the bill, which meant not only more business for the firm but more for the minter as well.

HOW JOINT VENTURING CAN CHANGE YOUR LIFE

There are a host of great benefits you'll experience when you joint venture. It goes without saying that joint venturing allows you to achieve advantages of scale, scope, and/or speed. You can take advantage of other people's infrastructure. You can take advantage of other people's reach. You can plug into a wealth of intellectual capital. And you can take advantage of other people's responsiveness, which, as a single proprietor or small-business owner, you wouldn't be able to do.

You can also enhance your competitiveness in local, national, and international markets because now you're in association with somebody who's a dominant force, somebody who has already built a market, or somebody whom your prospects already trust.

Joint venturing will also afford you the opportunity to enhance product development. You don't have to shoulder the burden of being the sole creative force in your company. You don't have to try to allocate an unavailable portion of your meager profits to doing R&D and coming up with breakthroughs for the future. Now you can just go out and find other people who have already done it and don't know what to do with it. Put their brilliant ideas through your distribution. Suddenly, you've got immeasurable flexibility. You've got a two-way valve.

With your newly installed two-way valve, you can take your product through as many different distribution channels as you like—publications, noncompetitive complementary providers of products or services, people outside your market, new applications of your product. And if you're gutsy, you can even go through competitive channels. Here's what I mean.

I partnered with another company that sold training programs to people on how to become a utility auditor or a real-estate property tax abatement specialist. The company's owners got tens of thousands of inquiries every year, but they sold only about 1,000 of them a $10,000 to $20,000 course. Ninety-five percent of the prospects making inquiries didn't ultimately purchase—but they were all interested in learning a skill. It's just that the skills this company was offering training on weren't the right fit.

So I got the owners to send a letter (one that I wrote and paid for) to all their nonbuyers, offering a program teaching how to be a marketing consultant. We got $10 million of business by mining that complementary.

Once you realize that you're not limited to just your own company product, you can create new businesses at will. You can get control of other people's distribution and other people's products. You'll become the link between two disparate businesses—and soon all three of you will expand. Process licensing, for example, is a gold mine; here's a great story.

I knew a gentleman named George who ran a lumberyard. He had a lumber mill, and he used it to cut, cure, and turn raw lumber into board, and then he sold the boards. The key to the whole process—the most critical function—is the kiln drying. If you make an error, your lumber goes from A-grade to reject. And if you do it wrong, you're not just wasting the raw material, you're also wasting tens of thousands of dollars a week on energy, on gas or electric. It's just a mess. But if you do it right, you save a lot of money and you get a premium for your lumber.

George did it right. He was a fanatic about it, and he had the best kiln-drying techniques around. The only problem was that the lumber business is inherently limited in terms of what markets you can tap into geographically. Lumber is so heavy that even if you wanted to literally give your lumber away to somebody 3,000 miles away, it would cost so much to ship that it wouldn't be worth it. From a practical standpoint, your market has to be consolidated within a 500- to 600-mile radius.

George came to one of my seminars, and I showed him how to take his kiln-drying method and license it to as many other lumber yards outside of his 600-mile competitive radius as he could, all over the world. Suddenly, he started making $2 million a year just from licensing a *process* that was already making him money in his own business.

Here's another example:

I worked with a dry cleaner who used what he learned from one of my seminars to develop incredible marketing to grow his dry-cleaning stores. Pretty soon, he had three shops in Chicago, but he didn't want to grow beyond that. He had this unprecedented marketing package with great specialty services, and he was earning about three times the average revenue of a dry cleaner, but that was good enough for him. His time was more valuable to him than money, so he didn't want the added burden of expanding further.

I respected that—but I told him there was no reason he couldn't increase his revenue in other ways, without adding more shops. I showed him how to license his incredibly lucrative marketing to *noncompetitive* dry cleaners—dry cleaners outside of Chicago. He got 3,000 dry cleaners to pay him $100 a month to use his advertising—and he became the maven of the dry-cleaning world!

The dry cleaner's story is an excellent reminder that there are two kinds of assets—tangible and intangible. With joint venturing you can get control of both, as this example shows.

I had a client who realized that companies with big telemarketing sales rooms tend to generate a fairly high rate of sales. Some of these companies sell business to business, which means that their marketing happens during the day. The companies that sell to consumers are normally telemarketing from 3 to 9 P.M.

My client was able to find business-to-business rooms that, although their owners had invested millions of dollars in them, were empty after 3 P.M. He leased these rooms on performance—based not on cash but on a share of the revenue. Then he went to consumer salespeople who wanted to leave their employers and start out on their own. He got equity in their business and a share of their revenue just for being the link between the company that owned the telemarketing room and the salespeople who needed the room. He made the money connection.

There are a lot of things that you can't afford to do, but if you joint-venture them and pay for them only in direct proportion to the revenue that comes in, they're no longer a cost. They're an income stream. They're a profit center. They're totally transformed.

And as a result, so is your business.

REAPPLYING OPTIMIZATION TO FIND HIGHER-QUALITY PROSPECTS AND CLIENTS

Let's return to an earlier example in this chapter, the misconception that increased sales are derived from increased contacts. Rather than turning 20 sales from 20,000 visits into 40 sales from 40,000 visits, you want to optimize the exposure you're already getting from those 20,000 contacts to convert more of them. You might even be better off getting only 10,000 visitors, if you get *higher-quality* visitors brought in by changing your message. You don't know which you really want until you try a couple of theories, which is very easy for smaller entrepreneurs to do—especially when you leverage the Internet.

The first leverage is to identify all the different possibilities that happen when visitors hit your website, and then see where you're losing them. My guess would be that you're losing them because the website is written about what's important to *you*, not what's important to *your clients*. This means that the path you want them to take through your website hasn't been strategically thought out from their vantage point. Put yourself in their shoes and walk through your site, or invite a client or prospect to do so and watch how she actually navigates from page to page. This second leverage is known as *usability testing*, and it can be an incredible eye-opener because it allows you to see how your clients actually use your site. It can help you confirm that each element of your website and step in your purchase progression yields a solid payoff value to your visitors.

Once you determine what is drawing in your users, you reverse-engineer the best parts. For example, you may be sourcing your leads from the wrong media or the wrong demographic, in which case you shift your focus to a better source. Or it could be the flip side: You may be sourcing from the right market but using the wrong bait (e.g., your message or keywords may be ineffective). You may even be sourcing from the right market and using the right bait, but when the users bite—meaning, when they hit your website—they're turned off by your message and leave without even digging further. This last scenario is so prevalent that it has its own term in the industry: the single-access ratio, or SAR. High SARs are the bane of every website.

The Internet isn't the only terrain where you can apply the theories of optimization to leveraging. Consider this example.

A few years ago I worked with a company whose owners were selling very expensive entrepreneurial/enterprise software. They ran ads in all kinds of trade publications and they got a lot of leads, but they converted very few of these into sales. I said to them, "Well, people who respond to these ads aren't doing it solely out of curiosity. They must want the benefit of enterprise software. They probably just don't want to spend $200,000 to $250,000; it's too expensive, too sophisticated."

So I proposed an idea. I suggested that they source some other software provider (someone with a lower entry-level version), get a license on it, and then offer that software to all the people who didn't buy the more expensive one. That's exactly what they did: They paid a 5 percent royalty to the other company, and then made three times as much on the people they didn't sell as on the ones they did.

It was the perfect case study of leveraging: The business owners didn't have to develop the software or pay for any of it; they just paid a royalty and let the people keep selling it themselves. And they made three times the profit they were making when they were going it alone.

Here's another example.

This one involves a Beverly Hills cosmetic surgeon—the same one I mentioned at the end of Chapter 9, who pioneered the infomercial in his field. He realized that everyone and their mother was advertising plastic surgery.

So he decided to write a book on the subject to position himself as the credible, preeminent source; instead of spending money on ads that didn't always convert, he ran a book promotion, which meant he immediately got money back when books were sold. Of course he also made a profit on lead-generating.

But how was he going to get his book out into the hands of the public? This is where he started looking for ways to leverage. The surgeon realized that one of the best, nonlinear sources of cosmetic surgery clients were the clients of other cosmetic service providers. So he hired a very attractive woman and mapped out a territory encompassing Beverly Hills and contiguous cities where other businesses offered cosmetic services. The saleswoman then called on high-end hair salons, high-end nail shops, and high-end spas—any place where people came and sat for thirty minutes or an hour—and offered to outfit the waiting room with a book. The plastic surgeon had done a thorough analysis of his metrics and knew what the statistical odds were: A scenario featuring 5,000 people a week sitting in ten cosmetic facilities reading this book was going to spawn cases. And it did. It can do the same for you.

THE JOYS OF JOINT VENTURING

Hopefully you now recognize the enormous potential of leveraging the talents and resources of other businesses, groups, and individuals. Joining forces with other unique and passionate people will take your business to dramatic new heights—a much better alternative than staying stuck isolated and alone.

Now I want to recap the major benefits that you can capitalize on by joint venturing. This is a golden opportunity, one you can't afford *not* to mine. So get motivated and act rapidly. Here are all the exciting ways that forming dynamic strategic alliances will revolutionize your business.

Joint Ventures Increase Your Sales, and Thus Your Profitability, Massively

If you're currently operating only linearly, with a single marketing activity/area or just a few, you might be making a living. But in tough economic times, just getting by might not cut it. Through joint ventures, strategic alliances, endorsements, and host/beneficiary deals, you could open up twenty new distribution channels or ten new markets that could increase your business by a factor of 5, 10, or 20. And if you can't handle that load, you can joint-venture with somebody who's got capacity and doesn't have sales. There's no problem, no need, no asset, no skill set, no issue imaginable that you can't access through creativity.

Let's say you wanted to reach the legal market, and you've never done this before. Well, you can cold-call attorneys. Or, you can find a trusted, successful company selling products or services or advice to attorneys that, although not at all competitive, has worked for the last twenty years building access and a reputation. Go to this company and make a deal that puts your offer through their distribution.

Lifetime value, which I briefly discussed in Chapter 9, refers to the totality of ongoing, cumulative profit that a type of buyer, client, customer, patient, or source is worth. Different kinds of buyers, and buyers coming from different sources, are worth a certain amount of money to you, not just in the initial sale but in their subsequent purchases as well. When you realize what that amount is, you can afford to invest very generously to acquire it. Here's an example.

In Chapter 9, I told you about how I helped Brian become a maven with his product, Icy-Hot. I'll clue you in now on another secret to Brian's success: He was able to take his company, which initially was bringing in only $20,000, and escalate it to $13 million in the next fifteen months by engineering joint ventures with radio stations, television stations, and publications—so that he *did not pay* for advertising. He let them sell his product, which was priced at $3 per unit, and keep all the money on the first sale. He transferred the dynamic and paid the media only for results.

People thought he was crazy, but Brian and I had done our math and we saw that every time we got two people to buy, one would buy every couple of months *forever*. And repeat clients would buy other products as well. Each such client was worth $30 in profit a year to Brian, for a lifetime. So every time Brian gave away $6—that is, two $3 sales—he got back $30 the first year and $30 every year thereafter for no cost at all. Now *that's* terrific lifetime value!

Joint Ventures Provide Added Value to Their (or Your) Clients

When you combine forces with another business, both of you can offer your products or services in conjunction with the other, so the client comes out with more benefits than she would have had if she'd purchased from you alone. Here's an example.

A martial arts club owner discovered he could give certain retailers valuable trial membership certificates to offer clients who made purchases at their stores. The certificates were good not for just one free lesson (which is typical) but for six full months of lessons, worth a total of $500. To the clients, then, the certificates had very high perceived value. So, the retailers could say, "I'll give you a $500 membership to this martial arts club if you spend $200 at my store."

One out of every four people who came in and redeemed their certificates ultimately became a $2,000 member. The retailers were delighted because they were able to add value for their clients; the martial arts club owner was delighted because he was getting incredible back-end value from the cooperation; and, of course, the clients were delighted because they got more bang for their bucks.

Joint Ventures Allow You to Enter Emerging Markets Instantly

Let's say there's a market that you don't know anything about, but you're eager to break in and be a pioneer. All you have to do is figure out who already has a presence in that market but isn't necessarily cutting edge.

Let's say that you've got software that's a breakthrough for bakeries, but you don't know anything about bakeries. Well, you don't have to find a cutting-edge bakery to offer your cutting-edge software to. Find a bakery supply company, a bakery consulting company, and a bakery equipment company and do a joint venture with them. That's how you can instantly usurp all the other people trying to enter that emerging market.

I've used joint venturing to take my brand to Asia, Australia, Europe, and Canada. I've used it to take my brand to the real-estate market, to the chiropractic market, to the martial arts market—and all with very little infrastructure. I used to have a big, complex infrastructure, but now I don't need that. I can accomplish all of my goals on a performance, soft-dollar basis. Why should I burden myself with huge overhead and an HR department? Let somebody else do all that—while I get the leverage off of it.

The potential for getting a foothold in international markets is especially exciting. I'm very proud of the following example.

When infomercials were just starting out here in the United States, I was doing seminars in Australia. Here's a classic case of OPM (other people's money), OPR (other people's risk), and OPS (other people's success): I taught an Australian direct-response salesman how to make millions of dollars in a way that, in retrospect, seems so shockingly easy that every reader of this book will wish he or she had been in this man's shoes.

Infomercials are expensive and risky to make, because you never know if a product will sell to a TV audience. But once you have a successful one, you can ride the wave of its success for a long time. So there are American infomercial makers who know which of their infomercials are making money. But they don't have outlets beyond the U.S. market.

Enter my Australian client. I taught him to approach the U.S. infomercial makers, respectfully suggest to them that they were limiting their horizon to just the United States, and point out that there are plenty of English speakers Down Under who would love to buy the products they were offering. I showed him how to get the rights to use their infomercials in Australia and New Zealand. He got access to infomercials that people were spending $400,000 to produce. All he needed to do was share (in a modest way) the profit from sales of the products in his territory. He made *$20 million a year* by getting the use of dozens of successful U.S. infomercials that had already been created and had proven successful. He didn't have to put a dime at risk creating products or infomercials. He just had to buy some TV time at 3:00 in the morning. Now, that's a win all around: The U.S. guys got a piece of a new market without having to lift a finger, and my client became very, very wealthy, thanks to his willingness to partner with others.

Apart from the limitless array of places you can go by partnering, it's OK if you don't have any infrastructure or capital! You know why? I'm sure you do by now: It's because you can access *anything* through joint ventures. Whatever you need—as long as you can show people that they'll get something great out of providing it for you—is always at your fingertips.

Joint ventures allow you not only to emerge into new markets but also to control other people's markets. Here's how this works.

Years ago, before the Internet had been developed, the way to communicate with people was through industry-specific advisor letters, or newsletters. I realized that a newsletter was the perfect vehicle for accessing specialized segments of the market, so I started typing up the rights to put inserts into other people's newsletters for no fixed cost, but for a modest share of the revenue.

The first offer I made to a newsletter publisher to tie up his insert rights didn't cost me a cent. I said to him, "I'll use your printer to print the insert, and they'll send me a bill." The newsletter publisher had ninety days deferred billing, so I got $30,000 worth of billing for my inserts that I didn't have to pay for ninety days. My first insert made me $500,000 long before then. I had to pay back $150,000 to the newsletter publisher, who owned the rights—but that was a fraction of what those rights were worth. I was able to capitalize on his biggest asset, because I thought innovatively and creatively.

Joint Ventures Give You the Opportunity to Share the Costs

Let's say you really wish you could penetrate new markets, but you've got to find a salesperson. The salesperson wants $100,000, and you don't have it.

If you're the one who's got the idea, you can go out and find three or four other (noncompetitive) people who want to reach the same market, and put the whole deal together so that they share the cost, give you a great ride, and you can build a sales distribution cycle. Let me give you a picture of what the flip side looks like.

Years ago, I had an "almost client." I say "almost" because the company went under before I could help it. It was a computer products company right when the big-box stores started selling computers for almost nothing, and it was getting squeezed. The company had about fifty salespeople, and it was doing $60 million in Southern California. The owners were trying to keep their heads above water by boosting their marketing. So, they called me in, but between our first conversation and the time I got the first proposal to them, they got cold feet.

I told the owner, "Please, if you'll just listen to me. . . ." I had found two people who were willing to pay him a six-figure up-front payment and one-fourth of the profits for the next three years to take over his salespeople. But he balked at the idea of waiting for future returns, was afraid to dig his heels in, and fired everybody without seeing where the joint venture would lead.

The moral of the story? The intangibles can be worth far more than the tangibles, but you've got to have the vision to see this.

If you have access to markets and you have a direct, implied, or explicit endorsement, and your competitors don't, three things happen:

1. The selling cycle is shortened.

2. The cost of access is reduced.

3. The response rate is enhanced.

That means you're going to sell more, you're going to sell faster, the cost is going to be lower, and you're going to make more money—even if you pay back a portion of that revenue to the endorser or the joint venture partner.

This is the power of the concept of lifetime value. Even if you pay very generously on the first sale but keep all the profit on the subsequent sales, you'll make out like a bandit.

Joint Ventures Give You Total Flexibility in the Way You Operate

My company normally has control of fifty different products and services at any given time that we're doing deals on in different forms in at least three continents at once—and I have only eight employees. If we had to do it all ourselves, it would take tens of millions of dollars. It would take staff. It would take specialists. Instead, whatever we need, we just find someone who's eager to be a performance-based, profit-based sharing partner, and we joint-venture. If the first one turns us down, we ask, "Why?" Sometimes they give us an answer that I had never thought about. So, I figure out a preemptive way to overcome that, and the second or third person I go to will be on board.

If you have a competitor who's weaker, instead of waiting for that competitor to go out, try a joint-venture type of acquisition. Show him how much better off he could be if he let you take over his clientele. Help him get rid of his overhead, release his offices—and pay him a share of the revenue on an ongoing basis. It's the best solution for both of you, but you have to shift your mindset to arrive at that kind of innovative and empathetic conclusion. The principles of joint venturing will give you the flexibility to get there.

Joint Ventures Are Less Risky

Say you're in Los Angeles. You want to open an office in New York? Great! But you've got to lease an office, and if it's a nice one, you'll be looking at a three- to five-year lease. You've got to furnish it. And then you've got to fill it with new hires. You've got to train them. You've got to buy equipment. If you've got a lot of money, no problem. If you don't, then it *is* a problem.

But what if you find a company whose owner is distressed? That is, she isn't using her opportunities fully, her relationships fully, her past clients fully. Imagine you could make a deal with her that's incremental, so it's variable-based. You just found a way to move to New York. But that's not all—you could be in Atlanta, Sydney, Tokyo, Toronto. And your downside is very little: If it doesn't work, you unwind it or you adjust it.

Sometimes, of course, it doesn't work because the money isn't good. Here's an example from my own experience.

I had a deal once with an infomercial company. The owners had done a large number of infomercials where they were splitting 50/50 on the revenue with the companies who hired them. About half the deals didn't seem to be profitable at first glance, and they summarily abandoned them.

I came in, looked over what was happening, and realized that a lot of the partnerships were back-end deals, meaning that once those companies got a buyer, the buyer continued to yield subsequent product/service revenue. So I told the infomercial producers, "Restructure the deal so that you show those companies that even if they made no profit and just got back their cost up front, they'll make money on the back end."

In other words, you can make a losing deal profitable. We renegotiated five of the deals right away, and suddenly the companies that had basically abandoned the relationship made a ton on the back end. I've said it before, and I'll say it again: It's all about your mindset.

Joint Ventures Give You the Chance to Access Knowledge and Expertise Well Beyond Your Company's Borders

There are so many consultants out there. There are a lot of excellent ones. And a good consultant really can make a difference for small- and medium-sized business owners. But most of the business owners who need them can't afford them.

Well, what if you could afford all the experts you ever wanted? There are three ways to make this a reality. Instead of paying for their specific expertise, you can convert their compensation to

1. a share of your results,

2. an interest in your company, or

3. an ownership in certain kinds of clients you acquire or sales you make.

I've also engineered deals in which I found prestigious experts, put them together as a board of advisors, and created a joint venture with them so that they had no liability. But when they lent their implied endorsement to my client, it gave my client preeminence and competitive advantage. And of course the advisory board got a share of new sales. This strategy has tripled and quadrupled profit margins.

Joint Ventures Can Strengthen Your Expertise in an Industry and Extend Your Product Offerings

I've done five joint ventures in the chiropractic industry: with three magazines, a cutting-edge technologist, and the leading chiropractic company. So now, if I send a letter introducing myself to chiropractors, they see me from five different impact points. My credibility, my stature, my attributes, and my relative worth are already pre-established because they're plugged in to the cumulative efforts and relationships of all these other people.

Then there's the issue of expanding your product line. Let's say you're a company that has one or two products but nothing else to sell. Find other related complementary or extended products, or even more advanced or expanded versions of what you're already selling, then sell those things and share the profits. You can find all kinds of other businesses, all kinds of other service providers, all kinds of other publications or associations that have a limited number of services or products and that need you as much as you need them. And even when the relationship is exhausted, that doesn't have to be the end.

Joint Ventures Can Provide Marketing or Selling

Let's say you've got a killer product, but you don't know how to market or sell. You joint-venture with somebody who does. Or the flip side: Suppose you know how to market or sell, but you've got no products or services. You know what to do. Here's a great story.

I had at one of my programs years ago the owners of a company that was in the aerobic attire business. They had really hot-looking clothing for people to work out in; however, their products numbered only about two or three, and they came to my seminar because the products were starting to slow down and they wanted to orchestrate a breakthrough. Upon asking some probing questions, I discovered that they had 5,000 to 6,000 retailers. They had Kmart before it got into trouble. They had a famous hosiery company with seven hundred outlets. They had Nordstrom's.

The owners were frustrated, but they weren't responding creatively. They had developed these two or three products, and that was it. I told them, "Your biggest asset isn't your product. It's your distribution and your relationship with the buyers. You can use that very advantageously. Go on a road trip to the hot cities: Chicago, L.A., South Beach, New York. Go to all the health clubs, and in their little snack shacks there's always some creative man or woman who's created a design for tennis shoes, or sweatshirts, or head bands. They're selling them at that health club, and nowhere else. Find those creators. Get a royalty deal on the product. Take it outside."

They immediately went into linear interpretation mode and answered, "We don't want to be a distributor." And I said, "Then don't be. Tell those designers they can keep all the sales from their one or two health clubs, and you'll give them a 5 percent royalty on all the other ones." The attire company owners were thereby able to tie up ten fantastic joint ventures that way—just by understanding posture, power, leverage, control, and the value of intangibility.

Joint Ventures Allow You to Stay Focused on Your Own Core Business While Expanding, Exploiting, and Harnessing Your Joint Venture

This one's straight from the Tom Sawyer School of Business. Do you remember when Tom had to whitewash the fence, and he got all the other kids to do it while he smoked a pipe and relaxed?

If you're able to take the fullest advantage of all kinds of assets, all kinds of distribution, all kinds of access that other people spent an enormous amount of time, money, effort, and credibility to establish, you can get functional control just by understanding what's out there, what it's worth, how to harness it, and how to communicate the idea to your prospective partner.

People ask me, "Jay, what's your theory of management?" And I say, "Don't manage. Do joint ventures." Plug into the resources of others, and they'll provide whatever you're missing. All you have to do is be the big thinker, the deal-maker, the strategist, and the visionary.

The biggest factor in harnessing joint ventures is the ability to become a more logical and more critical thinker. Collaborations are tricky by nature. It's rare that both parties operate equally—one will always have an edge. But if you remain focused on the intended outcome for yourself and understand that this will not be achieved until (and unless) you first help those on the other side gain the outcome they're after, you'll be surprisingly skillful and effective at making collaborations happen. It's all about the end result: In order for them to give back to you, they need to gain a meaningful outcome, too.

This is your time to experience exponential success—but that's not to say you have to go it alone. In fact you *can't* do it by yourself. Even if you could, why would you want to? The beauty of leveraging is that it makes life better for everyone involved. You'll experience success like you've never experienced it, profits far beyond those you garnered on your own, and a quality of life you've only dreamed of.

Looks like John Donne had it right all along: No man is an island. And no business is, either. Let the fruits of your fellowship commence.

The Bottom Line

- Entrepreneurism is about leveraging combined efforts. It's about helping other people get what they want so that they'll give and get you everything *you* want.

- If you believe that you have to do everything yourself, your business won't last.

- Break free from the "go it alone" mindset. It's no longer a value in today's business world.

- Good leverage is achieved when a businessperson takes action with the goal of producing a predictable, calculable amount of ROI. Bad leverage occurs when a businessperson takes action blindly, without knowing what ROI his activities will produce and only hoping for the best. Choose good leverage.

- Know when to expand and when to stay put. Start with optimization—getting the best from what you have—before you move on to innovation.

- When it *is* time to expand and propose a joint venture, take an assumptive role. Go in armed with your knowledge.

- The way to deal with a refusal of your joint-venture proposal is to empathize.

- When joint-venturing, avoid getting caught up in theory, starting out too big, or allowing yourself to be intimidated.

- Apply the theories of optimization to change the way you leverage. Increased sales do not come from increased contacts; they come from *higher-quality* contacts.

- The benefits of joint ventures are countless. Here are a few: They increase sales, provide added value to your clients, allow you to enter emerging markets instantly, provide you with opportunities to share costs, give you flexibility in the way you operate, lower risk, give you access to knowledge and expertise beyond your own limitations, extend your product offerings, provide invaluable marketing and selling conditions, and allow you to focus on your core business while expanding through the joint ventures.

☞ **Immediate Action Step** Drop everything and create one small, low-risk joint venture *right now.* As I've emphasized throughout, taking a shot at something trumps theory every time. And as Nike says, *just do it.* Don't postpone this, because if you do, you'll be among the 99 percent of business owners who are working too hard to make any real money!

11

HOW TO
GET GOING
AND GROWING
IN A
CRISIS ECONOMY

You did it. You just learned the nine sticking points, along with the secrets to getting your business unstuck in each area. And those lessons may have come just in the nick of time, too.

If you find your business facing a crisis economy—one like the sub-prime mortgage meltdown created in the fall of 2008—now is the time to capitalize on everything I've discussed. As you have seen, there are a number of factors that virtually none of your competitors will have the foresight and insight to focus on. After reading the previous chapters, you know what those factors are. Now you may be wondering, "Where do I start?"

In this chapter, I'll walk you through a synthesis of all the concepts we've talked about thus far. This is where we get into the nitty-gritty of how to get going and growing in a crisis economy. When we're done, you'll be armed with a creative, industrious, positive attitude in the face of hard times—the same hard times that cripple your competitors.

WHEN THE GOING GETS TOUGH, THE TOUGH GET GROWING

If you're reading this book in the middle of a crisis economy—and chances are pretty good that you are—it's vitally important to take careful stock of all the psychological and transactional changes going on in both the minds and lives of your marketplace and in the minds and lives of your competitors. We've talked a lot in this book about empathy, and for good reason. It's one of the most valuable tools you'll ever possess—for relating to the world at large, certainly, but *especially* when you're running a business.

Look at the attitude and actions of all your suppliers, vendors, and support services. You'll probably witness the following predictable reactions: Your competitors are feeling battered. Their sales and marketing approaches are generating meager results. They don't have a tried and tested plan of action. And they don't have a proactive strategy for capitalizing on all the things going awry. So, most typically, you'll see them pulling back and trying to cut costs to maintain a holding pattern. Or, they're redoubling the same ineffectual efforts that didn't really work during the good times but got masked by the upward force of the growing economy.

So what do you do?

Set up an offense and a defense. Offensively, you look for gaps, weaknesses, and hidden opportunity in all this adversity. And believe me: It exists in droves.

Defensively, you stop doing anything that isn't working. Implement the tools I empowered you with in Chapter 7: testing, monitoring, and measuring results. If you are super-vigilant, you'll know immediately when something isn't working, and you can stop wasting time and money on it right away. That saves capital by eliminating waste.

This will help you guard against loss, but you can do better than that. Your next step is to go beyond merely surviving and to begin enacting changes that will ensure that your business continues to evolve. So, begin to conservatively and safely test new approaches to replace the ones that weren't working and that you eliminated. In other words, you move from optimization to innovation. And in this kind of market environment, nontraditional approaches frequently prove the strongest. So instead of merely placing a better ad in the conventional paid media, you switch to finding the most direct and impactful way to reach and attract new buyers.

What are some of those direct and impactful ways? Well, we just talked about the importance of joint ventures in Chapter 10, so let's start there. Your first plan of action should be to structure joint ventures with groups who already have access, trust, and a credible relationship with the market segment you want to reach. This could mean going to noncompetitive businesses that are selling to the same buyer you're going after. It could mean selling something totally unrelated but selling to the same buying influence. It could mean going to anyone selling any product or service that your target buyers typically purchase directly before, right after, or at the same time they buy the product or service you sell.

Or it could mean finding your market's local, regional, or national association, journal, or organization and starting an endorsement deal in which it endorses, recommends, and tastefully promotes your product/service directly to its members. All these deals should be done on a pure performance basis whenever possible—which is most of the time—so that you pay the selling or endorsing source in direct proportion to the specific, actual sales that its involvement generates. You can also make similar arrangements with the sales force of any company selling directly to the same market you are targeting.

The key to this strategy is that it moves your costs from fixed and speculative to variable, contingent, and result-certain. But it gets even better. These steps comprise only Stage 1 of your "crisis growth" strategy. Your entire outlook and modified approach are based on gaining more direct, favorably predisposed, highly credible access to your market in unconventional (but highly ethical) ways—and these are ways that your competitors would never think to pursue. This is part of the strategy of preeminence we explored in Chapter 8: Make your product or service stand out head and shoulders above the rest.

Before we go further, keep in mind that, even in a grossly downturned market, not all sales dry up. Sales certainly can *drop* 30, 40, or even 50 percent. But people and businesses are still purchasing things. Commerce doesn't come to a full and absolute standstill. This realization is crucial.

Think about it. If a market normally does, say, 10,000 transactional purchases a month, and now it has dropped to 5,000, that sounds bad. And it is—for everybody else! In short, if you figure out how to gain preemptive access to those 5,000 transactions that are still alive and well, and you make irresistibly attractive offers through trusted sources, those prospective buyers will be all the more committed to you because you've offered them the solutions they need in a trying time. When your competitors are too blinded by their own panic to reach out to the marketplace in a meaningful way, that's when you have the best opportunity to establish yourself as the most trusted, reliable source. As I discussed in Chapter 2, instead of losing out to your competition your business can actually grow and thrive, while everyone else you compete against is bleeding red ink.

Following are some other strategies to use and implement.

We assume in a crisis economy that most conventional media stops pulling well. Unless you're crazy, you'd probably stop advertising there, right? But so would most, if not all, of your competitors, too! That means media advertising sales are down something terrible. And *that* represents a huge multiple opportunity for you. How and why?

First, when media sales are poor, media will make deals—and those deals can benefit *you*. You can undoubtedly get deeply discounted pages or radio or TV spots well below the nonprofitable rate that you and your struggling competitors were paying before the economy took a turn for the worse. And you know the adage: The key to profit in business is not selling but buyer rights. Remember that at a *higher price*, a one-page ad in a paper or trade publication or spots on TV or radio may lose you a lot of money. But *below* a certain price point, they suddenly turn into a real profit center. So you can renegotiate rates down, big time. Make certain, of course, that any deal you cut is discreet and comfortable and that you promise or warrant in writing to the media that you won't tell anyone about the great deal they're giving you. Here's an example.

At the time of this writing, a client of mine in the Southwest just made a deal with the major daily newspaper to purchase full pages, normally priced at $18,000 a page—for $3,500. My client and I need only one-sixteenth the normal response to break even. Can we get that, even in a bad economy? You bet we can.

Of course, even better than a low renegotiated price is a no-fixed price. You can engineer countless performance-based deals with the media when you are able to make them irresistible propositions. A key to success at structuring no-cost, performance-based deals is knowing your allowable cost for acquiring a new purchaser/buyer. Simply expressed, there are many factors involved in the anatomy of a sale:

- The profit available on the initial purchase

- The number of times that new buyers will most likely repurchase that product over the next year

- The number of years that the buyers will continue to purchase

- The additional products or services that the buyers will most likely purchase along with the main product, or instead of the main product, over the course of their buying cycle

- The profit those subsequent transactions will earn you over and over forever

As I mentioned in Chapter 9, this concept is called the *lifetime value* or marginal net worth of a new buyer. Once you have determined this value, you're in the catbird's seat to negotiate irresistible deals with the media on a purely performance basis. Here's how this can work.

Suppose, for example, you run a bottled-water delivery service and you know that a residential, $50-a-month new buyer purchases—on average—$50 a month every month for at least three years before he or she switches suppliers. In other words, every time you bring in a new, first-time buyer, this transaction is accruing or seeding for you twelve monthly purchases for three years, or thirty-six total purchases, each at $50. That's $1,800. Say your profit is 50 percent.

Armed with that knowledge, you could go to radio or TV stations or newspapers and offer them ads they can run whereby you let them keep $25 of every new sale the ads generate. If you have a good capital base or cash flow, you could offer them *all* of the first sale (or even more) and still make a big-time ROI over the next three years.

Most companies don't analyze what a lead, prospect, and converted first-time sale really costs them. But until you know that piece of information along with the lifetime value of the buyer, you can't go out and make killer performance-based deals with the media. By the way, I've made deals in which I gave the media 100, 115, even 200 percent of the first sale. And I always came out on top.

You might not have the cash to pay out 100 percent or more to acquire this future stream of income. But you can always find private investors who will put up the money to pay pure performance-based compensation to the media, for the advertising time, in exchange for the right to get their money out of the pot first (what's often called a "first money back-out-of-future profits"). That's how they get their investment repaid quickly and fully. You can even sweeten the deal by paying them an above-market interest on their money and giving them a kicker by sharing a small part of the profit for Year 1.

Ever been to the gift shop of a high-end health club and noticed that they had really distinctive handmade scarves or hats or something else lovely and expensive? Chances are good that the designer of those items lives within a few miles of the gym—and might even be a member!

If that expensive item is flying off the shelves in one big-city gym, in Dallas, for example, why wouldn't it be equally successful in high-end gyms in high-income neighborhoods in Los Angeles, New York, Boston, Chicago, Atlanta, and elsewhere? It would—but most designers don't have a marketing gift equal to their gift for creating beautiful things.

I taught one of my clients to travel around the country and visit the gift shops of all the high-end gyms and sports clubs, purchase unique items, contact the designers, and secure the rights to distribute them to the rest of the high-end gyms. It was a low-risk, high-reward proposition, because the items in question had already found acceptance from the discerning clients of a high-end gym—the very market my client was now pursuing, albeit on a larger, national scale. The result, to put it mildly, was very profitable.

Do you like that approach? What's not to like, when you encourage endorsers, joint venturers, or other companies' sales forces to generate new sales for you? Whenever you can convert unpredictable fixed costs into predictable, guaranteed-profitable, valuable, result-based investments, all the new sales/buyers your media joint venture generates will be pure profit.

And that's just one of the many exciting growth options I've got for you.

COMMANDEER A FRIENDLY TAKEOVER

Here's another approach. Let's look at your competitors. Some are strong, and those are usually the ones against whom you measure yourself. But what about the overwhelming majority of your lesser competitors, who are weak, and could collapse at any moment in an economy like this? Now, you could wait for them to fail, collapse, and go out of business and hope some of their buyers happen to migrate to you. But a better, more proactive strategy is to actually contact your weaker but respected competitors and offer to purchase their active buyers from them—for zero up front (so you're not risking a cent out-of-pocket). Instead, tell them you'll take over servicing or fulfillment of order/service requests and pay them an ongoing share of either the revenue or profits. You both win on this deal.

Here's why:

Say you're struggling competitor is in trouble and can hardly pay himself a salary. If you take over his *assets* (not his business), he can eliminate most, if not all, of his personnel, manufacturing, services, orders, client service, and so on. Let's say he has a $2 million business that's dropped down to $1.2 million. But his fixed overhead of staff and supply purchases is based on that $2 million sales level, so he's hurting terribly cash-flow-wise and may even be thinking about filing for bankruptcy.

But suddenly, you sweep in to save the day. You come in and offer to take over his buyers and service, putting them under the wing of your business. That means your competitor can eliminate up to 80 percent of his fixed overhead, sell all of his equipment, and sublease some or all of his facilities, thereby reducing his overhead/expenses even more.

By converting his buyers into your operation, you get to take advantage of the economies of scale and absorb his buyers into your system. So, for no extra cost to you, you pick up, say, 500 new buyers—which your current infrastructure and personnel can easily handle. Even if you pay your competitor 25–50 percent of the profit on all the buyers you acquire from him and you paid that split to him forever, you're still coming out great on the deal.

Plus, you're not limited to doing this with just one of your competitors. A client of mine did this with six different competitors in one year (one really bad year for his industry—but a great year for my client). His business tripled. And his competitors went from losing money to making more for doing nothing by receiving the monthly profit split checks he sent them.

You can even turn your competitors into star salesmen or saleswomen for you. How? Well, if you take over their buyers and show them how to eliminate most or all of their staff and reduce or eliminate their overhead, they're going to have a lot of unfilled time on their hands. What's more, they're receiving good money from you with no more overhead to use that revenue on. Your competitors are financially far better off. But now they're bored.

Many of those former fierce competitors started their once-prosperous businesses by being good to great salespeople, media generators, or networking masters. Unfortunately, though, a lot of beleaguered entrepreneurs stop doing what grew their business in the first place when they hit a certain size and instead start trying to be everything managerial. You can handle it differently: Once you've liberated those beleaguered competitors from the yoke of crisis, they are free to go out and start doing again what they originally excelled at doing—selling, networking, getting media exposure. Only this time, you get them doing it for you and your business.

Why would once-fierce competitors want to go out and generate new business and media exposure for *you*? Because, of course, you share all the profits that result from rechanneling their efforts. Those redirected "dynamos" can catapult your business into the stratosphere during bad times, once you help unshackle them from their own business strife.

Now here's the next strategy. One of the easiest "stealth" ways to grow a business that employs salespeople in a crisis economy is to start out clearly understanding and knowing your marginal net worth numbers. Why? Because once you realize the ongoing, recurring value and profit of bringing on a new, first-time buyer, you can easily embrace my philosophy of breaking even on the first sale. You start thinking about it as a long-term return on a one-time investment.

So, once you clearly know what the gross incremental profit (profit before all amortized overhead) after hard direct expense is for a first-time sale (whether it's product- or service-based), you can do something quite exciting. You can go to all your competitors' top salespeople and offer them 100 percent of the profit (or more) for all the accounts they bring you that you aren't selling now—if they switch employers and come to work for you (and stay with you a minimum validation period of time). Plus, you can give them a generous, above-current-level, ongoing commission afterward.

Why would you do that? For many reasons. First, most employers take their sales force for granted. They don't value the fact that the salespeople are the ones who build an entrepreneur's client base, revenue base, and income. The salespeople control the relationship; most buyers buy because of the salespeople rather than because of the company. Yet many companies treat their salespeople with ambivalence, even disdain. They push them when bad times come but fail to reward them for their achievements. Most entrepreneurs don't invest in growing their salespeople's ability and worth.

If you target your competitors' best salespeople and offer them super-attractive signing bonuses and above-market commission or pay, and if you commit to training them in *consultative selling* (see Chapter 3) and other professional development areas, they'll flock to you. Interestingly, most entrepreneurs do not have any kind of restrictive employment agreements, noncompete covenants, or protective arrangements in place to keep their salespeople with them. So you can have a field day by legally and ethically snatching away the top talent and real business builders from as many struggling competitors as you like. I once quadrupled a client's business in growth using this strategy alone.

A word of advice here: Whether you're going to approach your competitors directly about taking over their buyers on a permanent profit-sharing basis or you're going to focus on hiring away their top salespeople, you need to carefully plan your proposition, your presentation, and even the sensitivity/ empathy of your delivery. One of the keys to collaboration success is first recognizing exactly what those on the other side want or need most that is not being provided or achieved and showing them that your prospects, your plan, your strategy *will*—not can—deliver it to and for them in better ways, and more quickly and easily than any other option they have. Respect, acclaim, appreciate, and empathize with what they are going through first, so they will trust your intentions and plan.

The process is more extensive and detailed than just this— but the key to always remember is to put into words what your targets are feeling, struggling with, or desiring. Show them that you feel what they are feeling—that you know what they want and have a clear, safe direct path to get it for them.

Your next strategy: Make even more irresistible offers.

In a crisis economy, when sales are down along with buyer confidence or motivation, you need to make offers, propositions, and proposals that are irresistible, unbeatable, and non-refusable. And in this context especially, remember the lifetime value of the buyers. In any economy, your goal is to start the buyer relationship as quickly as possible, because the sooner they buy that first time, the sooner they'll come back and buy a second time, and so on. So your goal—whether in good times or bad ones—is always to lower their resistance, lower the barrier of entry, and reduce the hurdle. Make it easier for them to say "Yes, let's get started" than to say "No."

This goal is even more critical in a crisis economy.

How do you do it? You have a whole array of options. Consider one or a combination of the following:

- Extend such generous and irresistible risk reversals, trial offers, and money-back guarantees that people can't *not* at least try your purchase out that first time.

- Consider adding more bonuses, add-on products, services, or extended warranties to the purchase to make it such a great bargain that prospects can't possibly say "No."

- Figure out, when applicable, how to defer payment for your prospects or clients so they can have the product/service in their lives, home, or business *now* but not have to pay or start paying for it until later, when (ostensibly) the crisis conditions have improved.

- Provide far more support, follow-up, and benefit than usual to make your prospects and clients feel comfortable committing right away.

Another thing you can do is get your current suppliers/vendors, or new vendors who are eager to have your business, to provide assistance—perhaps in the form of funding subsidies to help you invest in more promotion and payments to partners for generating first-time buyers, media, PR, and so on. Remember the lesson of Chapter 6: Don't allow your costs to eat up all your profits. Here's an example.

In Chapter 2 I explained how my associates and I in the brokerage business got our investment companies to pay for full-page ads in the *Wall Street Journal*. Well, I've also gotten others to pay us to mail sales letters to our 500,000 clients, others to pay bonus "split" monies to our salespeople, and still others to pay for the creation and distribution of a hard-bound book on investing in bad times that we sent out to hundreds of thousands of prospects. Basically, I've gotten others to pay for *everything*.

If your vendors want to see you grow in bad times—to survive and thrive—ask them to invest in that process. If they're unwilling, consider finding vendors who have read this book and are willing. If you can't do that, buy a copy of this book for both, and go with the vendor who gives you the most enthusiastic and substantial offer of support!

PENETRATE NEW MARKETS

In a crisis economy, odds are great that your competitors are focusing their attention on the same basic market that all of you have targeted all along. If you move outside their radar, you can have a multitude of markets all to yourself.

Want some examples?

Say your business is home improvement. Business is down a lot. But select people are still doing home improvement. How do you find those people—before your competitors do?

Well, if everyone else is depending on either their newspaper ads or the Yellow Pages to generate business, you can tap into overlooked, undervalued alternative sources. For one thing, there's an economic connection between the incentive to do one type of home improvement and the incentive to do others. For example, people who re-do a kitchen suddenly see that the rest of their home looks old in comparison. So, they re-carpet and re-paint and re-do their driveway, roof, bathroom, and so on. It's the same for people who add a pool or spa. They re-do their landscaping, re-envision their garden, and add an extension to their back porch.

My point? Well, let's say you're the contractor remodeling a bathroom. You can go to all the people who do nonbathroom remodeling such as kitchen remodelers, carpet companies, and roofing people and make deals to get their clients' names after their work is completed. Their business is potentially a huge source of future business for *you*.

Remember: Even in a down market, business goes on. Business is down as I write this, but not everyone has stopped replacing their carpet. Not everyone has stopped re-doing their kitchen. Not everyone has stopped resurfacing their driveway. There will always be a portion of any marketplace with enough need or desire and financial capacity to do these things. Your job is to find out who they are, who they are dealing with, and how you can access them in the most direct, favorable, and cost-effective manner possible.

What's next? Look at your basic business—not at what you do sell but at what you *don't* sell that your type of buyer or client needs, wants, and will buy in a crisis economy. Most business owners see themselves as being highly specific sellers of a single category of product or service; yet the same people who buy from you also purchase complimentary or related products and services before, during, and after they buy from you. By adding additional back-end products or services that you can source from quality providers who, like you, are struggling in this crisis economy and will be open and willing to structure very advantageous deals in which you offer their products, you can double, triple, and even quadruple the revenue you earn.

So, go back and ask yourself, What else do existing buyers want or need? What else do unsold prospects or leads want or need to buy? If that "something else" is logistically related to what you do in your business, go out and source it (with a huge portion of the profit coming to you) and test out offering it to your people. I'd be surprised if it doesn't put a huge windfall of profit into your bank account right away, much less expand your ongoing business, revenue, and profits many times over. Here's a great example.

Tom Phillips is a mentor, friend, and former partner of mine. He's a brilliant entrepreneur. He took an idea and $1,000 and transformed it into a $450-million-a-year industry leader. How did he achieve this? In good times and bad times, he did three things every year, without fail:

1. Every year, he made certain that he penetrated at least one new market for each product or service he sold. This kept him far above the plateau of erratic business volume, which I discussed in Chapter 4.
2. Every year, he made certain that he introduced at least one new product or service to his existing buyers. Remember my discussion of strategizing techniques in Chapter 5? Well, add this one to the list—there's nothing your existing clients like more than new stuff.
3. Every year, he made certain that he acquired, usually on a pure performance-payment purchase basis, at least one new business he thought was perfectly suited to benefit off of innumerable infrastructures and buyers.

My friend Tom has mastered the art of growing his business regardless of what is going on in the surrounding world. His business always thrives—in good times or in bad.

Yours will, too, if you take action on my ideas.

The Bottom Line

■ Take stock of the psychological impact of the downturn on your competitors.

■ Set up an offense and a defense. Offensively, look for weaknesses and hidden opportunity. Defensively, stop doing anything that isn't working.

■ Begin to safely and conservatively test new approaches, such as joint venturing.

■ Measure your marginal net worth numbers. Once you determine how much a long-term customer is worth, you'll know how much you can invest in attracting first-time buyers and converting them to repeat buyers.

■ Now is the time to make deals with the media to get the word out about your business. They're primed to give you special treatment, because they're losing business too.

■ Offer your competitors' salespeople a better deal and get them on your team.

■ Negotiate friendly takeovers that benefit you and your competitors. But be sure to approach them with empathy and respect.

■ Make offers that are irresistible: Offer guarantees, trial periods, add-on products, and deferred payment plans. Provide even more support than usual so that your clients feel comfortable about committing.

■ Penetrate new markets while your competitors are busy focusing on their narrow niche.

■ Remember that not all buying stops in a downturn, even a severe one. If you can tap into the transactions that are still alive and well, you can not just survive but thrive.

☞ **Immediate Action Step** Lose the mindset that confuses "economic slowdown" with "economic total standstill." Yes, in a down economy, fewer people are taking the steps they would take in rosier times—putting in a new kitchen, getting new carpeting, taking a trip. Your competitor is going out of business because he possesses the mentality that says "No one's doing anything, period." Meanwhile, you're ethically and respectfully growing (and taking your competitor's business) because you are adopting the mentality that says "The pie may be smaller, but my piece of the pie is getting bigger and bigger!"

CONCLUSION

CONGRATULATIONS! YOU'RE UNSTUCK!

What is it like to be unstuck?

Imagine feeling in control of your destiny for the very first time. Your competitors and a faltering economy don't frighten you—they excite you, challenging you to conjure up innovative solutions. You see hard times as an opportunity for infinite growth, whereas your competitors cower in the corner, waiting for the sun to return. Meanwhile, you're ready to soar.

That time has come: You're ready now. The future is clear. You can predict what tomorrow will bring, as well as the next month and even the next year, because you now have a goal. You've established strategic processes for reaching that goal, and every business activity is launched with that goal in mind. Your business is working harder for you than you're working for it. You have multiple activities under way to source new prospects, and you have the necessary machine in place to migrate them through a long-term, systematic process that has no end. You've established methods to attract referrals of the highest quality and quantity, who will be moved through the same machine in good time.

You've identified new ways to reach your market and are constantly innovating to find even better ones. Your performance is always increasing, because you aim for constant improvement, with the objective of rendering your current model obsolete through innovation. You're consistently expanding your leverage through collaboration with a variety of resources, skill sets, and profit partners. You're spending significant time working toward the future, not simply trying to sustain the moment.

Your business is no longer stuck—it's growing. And it's becoming a prized asset, owing to its sustainable systems and predictable profitability.

In the previous chapters, we've identified and analyzed the nine reasons why businesses get—and stay—stuck, and we've seen what needs to be done in each of these areas to move off the plateau and into a dramatic upswing in profitability—and fun! We've explored the multifold advantages of leveraging—leveraging one's abilities, time, resources, and relationships. We've come to understand that success in the twenty-first-century business environment means the ability to collaborate creatively with others: No one individual can possibly know everything or have every piece of the puzzle.

Continuing to think that you *can* go it alone would be selfish, for three reasons:

- First, if you have a great product or service, you should contribute, because success is a by-product of contribution.

- Second, whether you are an entrepreneur or a corporate executive, your family is looking to you to make your business or career as fulfilling, low-stress, and asset-accruing as possible, for both you and them.

- And, finally, you owe it to your employees, investors, and other stakeholders to make your business as profitable as can be, because they, too, are counting on you.

Getting unstuck is about choosing the fastest and easiest ways to make a difference, so that your "wins" are realized.

This will animate your spirit, your sense of possibility—and your treasury! Your priority should be based not on the biggest payoff but on the question of which of these tools is easiest to implement right now.

As I suggested in Chapter 1, think of the Tin Man in *The Wizard of Oz*. He didn't have to go back to the shop in order to continue traveling down the yellow brick road. A little bit of oil, applied judiciously in the right places, got him moving again. That's what I hope we've accomplished over the course of this book: finding clear solutions that maximize results with the least amount of effort, and all the while enjoying the process. It won't happen overnight, but if you keep applying oil, you'll be headed toward a smooth and exhilarating future.

I have a very simple philosophy of life: You shouldn't steal from yourself. If you're going to commit your life to an enterprise, to wealth creation, and to the security and financial well-being of your family, and if other people—your staff, your team, your employees, your vendors—are going to commit their lives to you, you owe it to yourself and to everyone else to get the highest and best results. You should never accept a fraction of the yield when—with the same effort or less, the same people or fewer, the same time or less, the same capital or less, the same opportunity cost or less—you can gain so much more in this moment, and perpetually.

Destiny is yours for the taking. Even in a downward market, if you carry out the principles discussed in this book you will be in control. Of course, there will always be aberrations—in the economy, in world events. But you'll have far more control than any of your competitors, and it's their "stuckness" that will create a perfect opportunity for you to swoop in and claim the marketplace as your own. You can realize unhindered growth, knowing with certainty that you'll never, ever be stuck again.

So take that first step forward. Make the adjustments we've explored. Move from surviving to thriving, and on to the exponential growth that makes doing business a truly joyful experience for you and for everyone you serve.

The moment is now. It's time to unstick yourself! You can do it—easily, enjoyably, and very profitably. Seize your destiny—and leave the negativity and doubt to your competitors, as they surrender their clients to you. I'm rooting for you!

☞ **Immediate Action Step** Do something—anything! Right now! Before your competitors read this book. And let me know how it turns out. I'm always thrilled to see another entrepreneur reach new levels of success, and I want that person to be you.